SWINGING IN PLACE

SWINGING

JOCELYN HAZELWOOD DONLON

The University of North Carolina Press   Chapel Hill & London

IN PLACE

PORCH LIFE IN SOUTHERN CULTURE

© 2001

The University of North Carolina Press

All rights reserved

Set in Quadraat and Spontan Types

by Tseng Information Systems, Inc.

Manufactured in the United States of America

The paper in this book meets the guidelines for

permanence and durability of the Committee on

Production Guidelines for Book Longevity of the

Council on Library Resources.

Library of Congress Cataloging-in-Publication Data

Donlon, Jocelyn Hazelwood, 1956–

Swinging in place: porch life in southern culture /

Jocelyn Hazelwood Donlon.

   p. cm.

Includes bibliographical references (p.) and index.

ISBN 0-8078-2652-9 (cloth: alk. paper) —

ISBN 0-8078-4977-4 (pbk.: alk. paper)   FEB 2 5 2002

1. Southern States — Social life and customs. 2. Southern

States — Social conditions. 3. Porches — Social aspects —

Southern States. 4. Porches — Southern States — Pictorial

works. 5. Porches — Southern States — Folklore.

6. Interviews — Southern States. 7. Oral history. I. Title.

F209 .D66   2001

975 — dc21   2001027416

05 04 03 02 01   5 4 3 2 1

FOR MY PARENTS

Florence Materne Foreman on her porch, Lake Charles, La., ca. 1950.
(Photograph in author's possession)

CONTENTS

ILLUSTRATIONS

ACKNOWLEDGMENTS

Many writers begin their acknowledgments by recognizing that no book project is completed by the writer alone. But in the case of a book whose very subject matter depends on the willingness of people to tell their stories, a writer's debt to others is overwhelming and humbling. I begin my acknowledgments, therefore, to each person who so eagerly and generously contributed a porch story—and in several cases a treasured photograph—to this book. Saying "I couldn't have done it without you" is no cliché in this instance: it is a profoundly appreciated truth. Your stories have enriched my work and my life.

Many of these stories would not have come to me if Danny Heitman at *The Advocate*, Baton Rouge's daily newspaper, had not profiled my work on the porch and invited readers to contact me. I am thankful to Peggy Prenshaw for first suggesting that I contact Danny and for remaining supportive throughout this project. Kristin Svingen, at the *News and Observer* of Raleigh, North Carolina, helped me to broaden the scope of this work by putting out a call for stories in the North Carolina and Virginia region. For working his magic on photographs, I would like to thank Paul Bouy Jr. at Musemeche Photography in Baton Rouge.

For their readings and comments on sections of my manuscript, I wish to thank Sue Bridwell Beckham, Michelle Commeyras, Frank DeCaro, Marjorie Donlon, Karen Duplantis, Jay Edwards, Shannon McGuire, and Tom Rankin. I am also grateful to faculty members at the University of Illinois who contributed to this project's inception: to Alice Deck, who patiently trained me in discussions of race; to Larry Danielson, who gave me my first understanding of folklore; to Peter Garret, who said, "Your book should begin where you dissertation ends—on the porch," and was right; and to Michael Berube, who read early excerpts of this work with exceptional care. Their initial comments helped me to lay the foundation for this book.

I am indebted to Frank DeCaro and Rosan Jordan for inviting me into the fields of folklore and ethnography. Their invitation helped me to find my intellectual home, ultimately changing the course of this book. Their allowing me to teach undergraduate folklore courses at Louisiana State University not only deepened my understanding of fieldwork but also put me in contact with numerous students who have contributed their stories here. These LSU students were positively delightful to work with during my years as an instructor, and I am pleased to show them off in this book.

Jay Edwards has been indispensable in helping me to understand the architectural history of the porch. His many comments, his sharing of research, and his generous sharing of archival photographs have made this book much richer than it would otherwise have been.

Milton Rickels, my mentor at the former University of Southwestern Louisiana (now called the University of Louisiana-Lafayette), is responsible for helping me to find and to respect my professional voice. "Dr. Milton" passed away in 1997, but he remains very much alive in my work and in my teaching. He was the best kind of mentor, helping me to ask the tough questions while seizing the joy of scholarship. My debt to him is deep and abiding.

Elaine Maisner, my editor, has been invaluable. Knowing that I was writing for such an intelligent, careful, and supportive reader eased pains and worries too numerous and tedious to mention. To my family and friends, thanks for keeping the faith. To my grandmother, Florence Materne Foreman, thank you for having a porch worth remembering. To my parents, thank you for bathing my ears in stories since before I was born. My father, Calvin Hazelwood, graced me every week with storytelling in his sermons. My mother, Marie Foreman Hazelwood, blessed me by being an example of intelligence, compassion, strength, and wit. My sister, Karen Hazelwood Duplantis, reminds me each day of their legacy.

And, finally, to my husband, Jon Griffin Donlon, I want to say thank you. For over twenty years, Jon has been a perfect life partner. He has never foundered in his support of my work, and his confidence has carried me through several dark nights of the soul. His imagination, his intelligence, and his basic human kindness have made my life sweeter and my work richer. I thank all the powers that be that we have been able to make our journey together.

SWINGING IN PLACE

INTRODUCTION: WHY PORCHES?

I do not know when I developed a conscious appreciation of southern porch life. But I do know when I developed a conscious appreciation of being altogether southern—when I relocated from south Louisiana to central Illinois for graduate school. Before my northern trek, I had lived abroad for nearly a year. But Le Mans, France, for all its inscrutable social codes, did not offer some of the perplexing psychological hurdles that Urbana, Illinois, presented. For the first few weeks in the Midwest, I was confronted daily with unfamiliar dilemmas, particularly when it came to greeting others: Do I elicit eye contact with strangers, even though averting one's eyes is the local convention? If I believe I've seen this person before, do I nod and speak, simply nod, or feign lack of recognition until he or she speaks first? Throughout much of the South, it is customary to make eye contact with passersby and then to greet those people—perhaps several times a day. Hi, how ya doin'? *C'est tout. C'est normal.*

Thus I began years of drawing generalizations about southern and midwestern cultures. Not all midwesterners, I happily discovered, are hesitant to greet strangers. Nor do all southerners feel compelled to establish eye contact. Indeed, eye contact has been an emotionally charged, sometimes devastating custom throughout southern racial history: African American men of the Jim Crow era were sometimes lynched when whites accused them of greeting the wrong white woman at the wrong time and place (see Goldfield). "All Southerners are not alike," Margaret Jones Bolsterli has said, in her memoir *Born in the Delta: Reflections on the Making of a Southern White Sensibility.* "There are many 'Souths,' but there is something common to all of them not found in other regions of this country, and Southerners tend to think of themselves as having been shaped by 'place'" (4).

There are many Souths, and, while claiming cross-cultural practices as belonging to the South as a whole, this work attempts to recognize complexities and differences within the region. What's more, many different places have shaped southerners, places that can be as varied as southerners themselves. Certainly, though, the house porch endures as a cross-cultural site of real significance throughout the South. Much of my own "southernness," particularly my penchant for greeting, undoubtedly owes something to my grandmother's Louisiana porch. Admittedly, her porch has not been the sole determinant in shaping my social practices. Simply going to the grocery store in much of the South often requires conversation with, at the very least, the cashier. And certainly my being the daughter of a Southern Baptist minister imposed some sense of sociability on my family and me: We were expected to be "on" for others and to "remember who we were." But what my grandmother's house taught me was that by merely occupying a porch, an individual acknowledges her connection to the community at large. At the very least, porch dwellers are compelled to greet passersby, familiar or strange.

Rose Anne St. Romain, a professional storyteller from the central Louisiana town of Mansura, tells the following story about the custom of greeting others from a front porch. When, as a child, Rose Anne made the journey to nearby Plaucheville to spend the night with her grandparents, she would join them in their daily porch ritual. After having put on fresh makeup, Rose Anne's MaMa would sit on her front porch simply to wave to the people of Plaucheville as they drove by. According to Rose Anne, "That porch-sitting ritual happened *every* afternoon. I thought it immensely boring, but my grandparents were quite dedicated to it. And I always wondered why MaMa would freshen her makeup and lipstick when the people in passing cars were at least 300 yards away!" Her story continues:

> I remember spending a lot of time as a kid with MaMa. I spent a lot of time over there. One time she said, "Well, let's go sit on the porch."
>
> I said, "What are we gonna do?"
>
> She looked at me kinda quizzically, and she said, "Well, we're gonna greet passersby."
>
> I said, "And then what are we gonna do?"
>
> She said, "We'll wave."
>
> And she and my grandfather would sit and rock. He had his coffee can — he chewed tobacco — and he would spit, and rock, and wave. And when a car would come, MaMa would kinda crane her neck a little and watch . . . and wave.

I'd say, "MaMa, who was that?"

"I'm not sure, my sha." *

"Why did you wave?"

"Well . . . you *always* wave!"

Indeed, "you *always* wave" is a lesson taught early to many southern children. Nell Coleman, who grew up in Brookhaven, Mississippi, is among those who recognize this abiding "need to greet" in the South. She said to me in our interview about her family porch, "You could go up to Brookhaven this day, and you won't know a soul up there. But everybody that you will meet on the road will wave at you." The cultural norm of greeting is not by any means dead in the South. And certainly the front porch has helped to institutionalize this social practice. The porch, however, has done much more for southerners than encourage waving and greeting.

African American poet Frenchy Jolene Hodges begins to speak to the porch's cultural significance to the region as a whole in her poem "Belle Isle: (Central Park of Detroit)":

> In the South
> Where I come from
> All houses have front porches
> And most houses
> Lay claim to back porches too.

From the outset, Hodges speaks to the importance of southern porches by celebrating their ubiquity in the region. She continues her poem by calling the porch a "breast-pocket / of a family's up-and-coming-ness / Or down-and-outed-ness," indicating its class functions. In this poem, the porch is a vantage point for seeing "the world go by" and one where individuals, too, can be seen; the porch is a place to court; and it is a place to tell stories:

> If-you-do-this-that'll-happen-stories,
> The-dead-who-visit-the-living-stories,

---

* "Sha" [pronounced with a short "a" as in "shag"] is Cajun French for "dear," deriving from the French "cher."

Daddy-you-made-it-end-wrong-stories,
Tell-that-one-again-stories,
That-don't-make-no-sense-stories . . .

Like Hodges, my own storytelling history, my sense of cultural identity, and my connection to the South, itself, owes much to a house porch, particularly my maternal grandmother's porch in Lake Charles, Louisiana.

Indeed, because this work is stimulated by my personal experience, I have, in the remainder of the book, occasionally included stories from my own life as well as stories told by members of my extended family. Incorporating the personal into academic writing is a subject of much debate. Recently Rita Felski, in questioning her own lack of desire to incorporate the personal, posed the following question: "What authorizes the discourse of personal criticism? Why is writing about oneself deemed important or interesting?" (33). For this project, my personal experiences are essential to the discussion because they go to the very heart of it. When I am asked, "Why porches?" the first answer that comes to mind is "because my grandmother had one, and it has been a powerful influence in my life." Her porch has also been a powerful influence in shaping this book and thus warrants some attention here.

In the 1960s, when I was coming of age, my family would journey three or four times a year to my grandmother's working-class neighborhood in Lake Charles. Whenever my immediate family of seven arrived, we would sit on the porch, several of us occupying the swing that my grandparents bought when they got married in 1908—a porch swing that they moved from their home in Moss Bluff, a settlement outside of Lake Charles, to "town" around 1940, a porch swing that, when my grandmother died in 1977, my own father claimed in order to guard his memories of having courted my mother on it. Until my grandmother, Florence Materne Foreman, passed away, her front porch was significant to our family life, even when we weren't literally at her house, on her porch.

Part of the broad significance of my grandmother's front porch came through the stories my mother told. Before she passed away in 1997, my mother, Marie Foreman Hazelwood, frequently recalled porch memories of family and community. She talked of how she and her family would, on hot summer evenings, burn old rags to keep the mosquitoes away while catching up on stories. She recalled how she and my dad courted on the front porch swing. She even talked of the porch's political significance in the following story about the election returns of 1932, the year Franklin Delano Roosevelt was first voted into office:

> One of my earliest memories—when I was about four or five—was when I first heard the presidential election returns broadcast over the radio. We were one of the few families in Moss Bluff who had a radio, so Daddy moved it out on the porch so that a lot of our relatives—Aunt Della, Uncle Mip, Aunt Cecile—and a lot of people from the community could come over to hear the returns. There must have been about fifty people there, standing on the porch, where the radio was set up on a long table. When Roosevelt won, they played the song "Happy Days Are Here Again," and it was the first time I ever heard that song. Every time I hear it I think about that night that Daddy moved the radio out on the porch. . . . And it bothered me when they didn't play the song at the convention this year [1992].

My mother's story speaks of how her family extended itself to the community of Moss Bluff by way of porch events. My grandparents invited onto their front porch people who had been hard hit by the Great Depression so that they could await together the coming of new political promise. This story is one among many about my grandparents' generosity: stories about their lending their automobile for people in Moss Bluff to get to the doctor; about my grandmother, her sister, and my uncle building coffins and sewing burial shrouds for members of a separate black community dying in an epidemic; and about my mother's older brother Elray, who was exceptionally tall, being made to lie down in the coffins built for these dying people to test their length (a story that always makes me wonder just how gothic Faulkner really is).

My mother's porch story is traditionally southern, governed by norms of sharing with the community: She was taught to reach beyond herself to give to others. The story begins to explain why she eventually married a minister and chose to spend her life in service. She was unsettled by the Clinton/Gore break with Democratic tradition in 1992, when they did not play "Happy Days Are Here Again," because the song connected her back to that childhood porch where her earliest memories rested, where her identity as a southerner began.

In the 1960s and 1970s, when my family would go to my grandparents' house (after they moved to town), the porch was the center of our extended-family life,

Hazelwood family farm, Opelousas, La., 1980. (Photograph by Jon Griffin Donlon)

particularly for the children. The inside of the house was small—probably less than seven hundred square feet—and our family was large. We often visited in the summer. My grandmother detested air-conditioning, so the porch was an escape from the throngs of people sweltering indoors, where my grandmother had her eternal pot of beans simmering.

We spent endless hours on this porch, bounded by pink and blue hydrangeas that bloomed on the same bush, by lush crape myrtles with fuchsia blooms, and by a mature chinaberry tree that provided us with shade. Sometimes the countless children—my siblings, our cousins, their friends—would pile into the swing. With utter disregard for the rich history of that porch swing, we would recklessly test its limits to see just how high it could go and just how many people it could hold. The adults obviously showed a remarkable lot of tolerance for the remark-

The author and her husband, Jon Donlon, on their Spanish Town porch,
Baton Rouge, La., 2000. (Photograph by Jon Griffin Donlon)

able lot of noise and chaos we managed to generate. Even though we children often believed that we owned the space, I do remember our having to defer to adults. When aunts, uncles, adult cousins, friends, and acquaintances claimed the porch, children either fled to another place or became "story listeners" on the fringes of the porch while the adults occupied the swing, the wooden rockers, and the red and green, shell-shaped, rocking metal chairs.

My grandmother's porch did occasionally give way to privacy, transforming itself into a place of calm and solitude. Because I was the youngest child in my family, I often went alone with my parents to what became "Grandma's house" after my grandfather's death in 1963. I have fond memories of situating bed pillows comfortably on the porch swing in order to nap in the warm-to-hot Louisiana breeze (when there was any breeze at all).

During those quiet times, my father, Calvin Hazelwood, often spent time in reflection on my grandmother's front porch. I wish now that I had pressed him for his thoughts, but his death in 1980 closed such conversations. There's a good chance that he wasn't thinking conscious thoughts at all but simply seizing on the all-too-rare tranquility. There's an especially good chance that he was pondering his next sermon. Perhaps he was recalling the family porch on his parents' farm in Opelousas, Louisiana. I like to imagine that he occasionally remembered the following story about his daddy, Lewis Howard Hazlewood (my father changed the spelling of his surname to "Hazelwood" because he grew weary of correcting people), a resolute Southern Baptist deacon. The following story was told to me by my father's younger sister, Ottie Hazlewood Mercer:

> I remember sitting on our porch, listening to Daddy, as he helped one of our employees, who was pastor of a little church for blacks down the road that Daddy visited a lot—that we all visited a lot. I think his name was Joe. He would select his text, and then he and Daddy on Saturday afternoons would talk about what text he was gonna preach on the next day. I realized then what a Bible scholar my daddy was. We had to be quiet if we joined that group because this was serious business as far as they were concerned. But it was kind of a privilege, too, to be allowed to sit there and listen.

As is so often the case with porch stories, Aunt Ottie's story reveals a wealth of family history and culture—the sharing of knowledge, particularly biblical knowledge, with others; the central place that the Southern Baptist church still occupies in my father's family; the loving but firm discipline of my nearly legendary grandfather, who passed away before my parents were married and whom we knew primarily through my father's sermon illustrations of him; and the deep reverence and gratitude for the entire spiritual setting. The porch here is a place for the family to exercise its values and to influence others. Indeed, I do like to imagine that on the tranquility of his mother-in-law's porch, my father, as he contemplated his sermons, called to mind the lessons taught to him on his own childhood porch.

I never enjoyed a porch of my own until my husband and I purchased an older home in Spanish Town—a bohemian neighborhood in downtown Baton Rouge—in 1996. I have always thought it significant that we submitted the bid for our house on June 24, my grandmother's birthday. In spite of a twenty-five-year gap in my porch life, I nevertheless consider myself a "porch person," most likely inspired by the influence of my grandmother's porch. On her porch, I learned much about extending community boundaries—and also about setting them.

PORCH BOUNDARIES

With the appearance in 1702 of the first gallery in Old Mobile (Oszuscik 1), through its widespread popularity in the nineteenth century, and until its ebb in the 1960s after the ascendance of air-conditioning, the porch has served as "a shady transition between indoors and out" (Moore, Smith, and Becker 24). In addition to providing a relaxing, shady place to escape indoor heat, the porch is a social site for watching the community go by, a comfortable spot "where one [can] relax and sip iced tea, talk with a friend on the swing, or eat summer suppers" (Moore, Smith, and Becker 24).

But celebratory as southern culture can be, particularly southern porch culture, I want to clarify that I am not writing solely to romanticize the nostalgic side of southern porch practices—though I attempt to do as much celebrating as possible. Denying the less romantic side of the porch would be folly, to say the least. Much of what has contributed to the development of "many Souths" has been the sustaining—and the occasional crossing—of boundaries, be they boundaries of class, race, gender, sexuality, or even of generation. And the porch, as so many of the informants' stories in this book illustrate, historically has helped to institutionalize those boundaries throughout the region.

Indeed, while my grandmother's porch was about creating intimacy among family and friends, it was also about setting boundaries with "Others." In the late 1960s, after my grandfather died, my grandmother's neighborhood made the transition from a working-class white to a working-class black neighborhood; for the last decade of her life, Grandma lived as the only white woman in her community. Thus, her swing, which had rocked us in an all-white community, was now supporting us in a black one. Her porch became a metaphor for the transformation of social systems in the South. My grandmother interacted with her neighbors from day to day. Her porch was a place of limited racial interaction, where her black neighbors would stop to speak or where members of the black community in Moss Bluff who remembered her having sewn burial shrouds for their dead occasionally visited to see if she needed anything. However, when we all arrived as a white family, the boundary lines between "us" and "them" seemed to be drawn automatically.

Introduction

It was during this period of the neighborhood's racial transformation that I came of age to swing to stories being told on my grandmother's porch. I have already said that my grandmother's front porch shaped, in large part, my southern notions of community. In particular, the porch shaped my notions of racial communities during the turbulent period of desegregation in the South. And Grandma's porch gave to me a new racial vista. Even while I was participating in my own heritage, this porch provided me with a safe arena, a territory of family from which to view the public goings-on of the black neighborhood. I was quite often conscious that our activities on the porch were circumscribed by a black community—that we, for once, were different. I cannot say that there was any genuine sense of community with the people living nearby, since they were, from my family's perspective, positioned more as *objects* for our curiosity and observation rather than as other individuals with whom to socially interact—much as our family may have been perceived by the neighbors. But while I cannot remember ever socializing with the black children in the neighborhood, we were taught to be polite, to wave and greet, and to remember to behave. This was, after all, my grandmother's neighborhood, and she had to live there after we left. Ruth Frankenburg, in her book *The Social Construction of Whiteness: White Women, Race Matters*, has talked about the dominating, presumed universality of whiteness. She says, "'Whiteness' refers to a set of cultural practices that are usually un-marked and unnamed" (1). But on my grandmother's porch, our whiteness was very much perceived, marked, and named as the boundary lines were drawn.

Frenchy Hodges's poem offers a glimpse of these racial boundaries from the African American side. She says that front porches are places where "the neigh-borhood" can be viewed and celebrated. They are places where people can sound traditional African American songs:

> Swing-Low-Sweet-Chariot-Another-Man-
> Done-Gone-We-Call-The-Sun-Ol'-Hannah-
> Swing-Dat-Hammer-Sometimes-I-Feel-Lak-
> A-Motherless-Child-Mighty-Lak-A-Rose-Songs.

These front porches are where an African American community can extol and protect a separate community identity. But, like it or not, they are places that often intersect with the dominant white world. They are places:

Where the old ones
Made sure you knew
Who you were
And who they were
And what "white" was.

Hodges, claiming that front porches hold special value for African Americans because they are "the revolutionary cribs / Of [her] race," concludes that porches are "very important places" (5–8). And indeed they are. My grandmother's porch, though I haven't sat on it for over two decades, has been integral to my identity as a white, lower-middle-class southern woman. So much of this book is about race—from a white perspective—because my grandmother's porch was inextricably tied to race; so much is about family because I cannot separate my grandmother's porch from family; so much is about everyday work activities because I never saw my grandmother not working on her porch. I fight against nostalgia because my own view from the porch often belied its romance.

Such personal experiences have affected not only this book's structure, but also the results of my fieldwork. In my interviews with others, the initial questions I posed often sought to evaluate their experiences against my own. As I listened to others in interviews and read the letters written to me, I inevitably questioned my preconceptions about the porch. The final product, then, is a synthesis of my own observations and those of people who shared their stories with me, either in letters or in interviews. Together, we set the terms for this study of porch life in the South.

1: SETTING TERMS

On April 26, 1998, an article written by John Woestendiek appeared in Baton Rouge's *Sunday Advocate* reporting that on July 1, 1998, the town of Wilson, North Carolina, would "begin inspecting neighborhoods, ordering fines, and removing items that violate health and aesthetic standards." The items that allegedly would "violate health and aesthetic standards" were pieces of indoor furniture, namely upholstered sofas and chairs, that had been relegated to front porches. The ordinance, which was passed by the Wilson town council on March 19, 1998, predictably set off a battle between social and economic classes in the small town (D4). According to a 1998 article in the *Economist* titled "A Man's Porch Is His Castle," about one-fifth of "Wilson's 40,000 residents are poor. Their homes, some of which are heated with coal, stand a few blocks from the baronial piles of Wilson's most prosperous citizens. Of the 15,000 houses, apartments, and trailers, almost half are rented. . . . As it happens, it is blacks, in the poorer central part of town, who tend to have the rickety furniture on their porches. Another southern tradition may therefore be in play: stern paternalism imposed by the mostly-white haves on the mostly-black have-nots" (31). Those who made use of indoor furniture on their porches claimed that the town council should "be worried about feeding the poor people, not what they have on the porch." But an editorial in the local newspaper said, "The South has many great traditions . . . but litter in yards, parking on lawns and indoor furniture being used outdoors are not the benchmarks of Southern culture" (qtd. in Woestendiek D4).

John Shelton Reed, in a 1998 column for *Reason*, went to the heart of the matter:

There's a class angle to this, of course. Like much of the South's traditional culture, porch sitting survives in its least self-conscious form among poor and working-class folk, black and white. It isn't the country-club set, after all, who enjoy waving as the cars go by. Moreover, these are the same folks who often can't afford air conditioning or cable TV. The problem, as the Appearance Committee sees it, is that they often can't afford decent-looking porch furniture either—or at least that they see no reason why they shouldn't furnish their porches with beat-up old sofas or recliners that have outlived their usefulness in the living room. (51)

As Reed indicates, the town's battle over "appropriate" porch furniture signifies how the front porch does much more than offer, at 92°F in the shade, a relatively cooler place to greet passersby or to swap tales. Wilson's community conflict illustrates how the porch can both connect and divide community members: Neighbors can be involved in each other's lives because of the porch, but they can also feel compelled to assert their class distinctions and social preferences when it comes to making "appropriate" use of this domestic space, which is at once personal and public.

Socially, politically, and psychologically significant, the porch is a charged transitional space between public and private spheres. Facilitating yet limiting access to others, the porch inextricably links community members to each other, while setting boundaries—be they boundaries of class (as exemplified in the Wilson ordinance), of race, of gender, or of generation. Indeed, what fascinates me most about the porch is how it helps to set the terms of a community, how it fosters the policing of boundaries—boundaries that separate "private" from "public," "self" from "other," and "home" from "community." In essence, the porch creates a "liminal" space.

LIMINAL SPACES

By bringing together "the porch" and "community," I am exploring both spatial and social practices. As geographer Edward Soja has termed it, I am looking at "the social production of space" (136). A key phrase for this exploration is "transitional space." Every student of folklore and anthropology knows of Victor Turner's discussion of liminality—a discussion that was informed by the work of French ethnologist and folklorist Arnold van Gennep. "Limen" is Latin for "threshold"; thus, liminality is an "in-betweenness," a condition that allows a person participating in a ritual performance to disrupt traditional norms and expectations and to enter—sometimes temporarily, sometimes permanently—

a state that is "neither here nor there" (Turner 232). Liminality is thus a "gap between ordered worlds," where individuals, during the ritual process, are "liberated from normative demands" by being ambiguously situated between, not within, social systems; they are in a kind of limbo between sacred and secular worlds (Turner 13). Sue Bridwell Beckham, in her 1988 essay, "The American Front Porch: Women's Liminal Space," expanded Turner's work on liminality by applying the term to a physical space. Recognizing that the porch is "betwixt and between absolute private and absolute public" (75), Beckham broadened the concept of liminality to include the physical, as well as the psychological, realm of individuals.

The porch indeed constitutes the quintessential liminal space—as confirmed by my own two cats each day. Until 1996, W. C. and Camilla had been indoor cats for more than ten years, with, alas, no porch to call their own. But when my husband and I bought our home in Spanish Town, we acquired a screened-in front porch, which we thought would be a perfect berth for our now elderly, extremely lethargic, fat cats. Our cats, however, had become so conditioned to living indoors that for weeks they cowered like proverbial "fraidy cats," tarrying strategically on the threshold between indoors and out, "neither here nor there," sniffing the outside air of the world unknown to them, yet taking refuge in the familiar territory of the inside. Even today, they are not comfortable on the porch unless we leave an interior door open for them, through which they can hightail it back into the house at the sound of any menacing noise.

Liminality is so fundamental to the nature of the porch that even my cats respect it in their maniacal patrolling of the threshold. But humans are also inclined to practice such policing, on the same kind of visceral, almost instinctive level. This observation might be particularly true in Spanish Town. Our neighborhood includes residents of every make and model, an assortment of people who can occasionally make some visitors, even other residents, uncomfortable. The architecture is late nineteenth and early twentieth century, so porches abound in Spanish Town. These porches offer handy positions from which to spy on the eclectic collection of people, even as they encourage brief, nonthreatening visits with many different kinds of folks. Indeed, Martie and Mike Richmond, who live in a pink shotgun house on Spanish Town Road, call this home their "urban camp." They own a home in a more industrialized section of Baton Rouge, but they bought the shotgun house to spend their weekends "camping" in our neighborhood, visiting with their neighbors, and knowing that when we host the Spanish Town Mardi Gras parade each year, they and their friends will have prime viewing positions from their porch. In fact, the Richmonds recently moved into the shotgun home full-time in order to restore a larger house in Spanish Town, which eventually will become their permanent residence.

Because porches allow for a renegotiation of the rules, new, if temporary, relationships can be created. As Sue Beckham has said, "Relationships that would be impossible elsewhere can flourish for however brief a time—and they can be spontaneous" (75). I believe this kind of relationship existed with my grandmother and her neighbors, as well as with those members of the black community near Moss Bluff who survived the deadly epidemic. Most of these visitors from Moss Bluff were black men, and during the days of intense racial segregation, I suspect that my grandmother would probably not have established lasting relationships with people of different races, had it not been for her porch. The liminality of the porch, which temporarily modified the rules of racial segregation, allowed for the connection between my grandmother and people of other races to be sustained and even to flourish, while it nevertheless enforced the boundaries of the threshold. In essence, this porch became a "creolized space."

Closely related to the term "liminality" is the word "creolized." Because it is a liminal place, the porch has a hybridizing effect, bringing together a mix of peoples and cultures to rearticulate the rules of a larger culture; the porch thereby becomes "creolized." Indeed, as I trace it more fully in Chapter 3, the porch's history is a creolized one, drawing from Haitian shotgun houses, African traditional architecture, Indian bungalows, and opulent classical porticos. The various names for the structure indicate that it comes from many different origins. Jay Edwards's article, "The Evolution of Vernacular Architecture in the Western Caribbean," traces the ways in which the different architectural terms reflect the diverse origins of the extended house porch. "Veranda" is believed to derive from the Hindi *vara*, which means "to surround with poles"; "gallery" derives from the Italian and medieval Latin and is used in French colonial regions; and "piazza" has its origins in Italian to signify an open town square. "Porches," which are not full-facade, derive from seventeenth-century European models (325). As we

Martie and Mike Richmond and friends on the porch of their shotgun house in Spanish Town, Baton Rouge, La., 1999. (Photograph by Jon Griffin Donlon)

will see in more detail later, this history verifies that the porch is "a creolized phenomenon" (Vlach, *Afro-American Tradition* 133).

At this point, we can formulate several questions. How does the liminality of the porch make use of established social pressures and conventions? How does the porch's in-betweenness contribute to the shaping of a person's identity within a community? How does the porch facilitate the creolization of cultures? How does the porch function not only in terms of class, race, and gender, but also in terms of sexuality? The porch, after all, is entrenched in heterosexual traditions of courtship. How does the porch shape a family? Does it provide cohesion? Is it an escape? At the most fundamental level, what kinds of daily activities does the porch encourage? And do these activities and practices vary from culture to culture, or from region to region, throughout the "many Souths"?

To answer these questions, I have spent the last several years collecting letters written to me by southerners who want to share their porch memories, as well as interviewing people who grew up with front porches that were significant to their identities. I have made a substantial effort to communicate with as many different people as possible—black, white, rich, poor, gay, straight, male, female. Because of my own geographical constraints, the majority of my informants are now living in southern Louisiana. However, many of them grew up in other southern states, particularly in Mississippi. The letters I received were largely in response to Danny Heitman's coverage in the Baton Rouge daily newspaper, *The Advocate*. In 1996 Heitman profiled my research on the porch and invited readers to record their memories for inclusion in this work (September 21). I want to clarify that, although many informants came forth from the Baton Rouge area as a result of the newspaper coverage, the people who responded in writing are not necessarily my personal acquaintances, and they should not be construed as representing a limited community of informants known to me. Kristin Svingen also profiled my research in the *Raleigh News and Observer* (August 6, 1999). Following this coverage, I received several letters from people in both North Carolina and Virginia, and those stories are also recounted here.

To look further at porches, I have included several literary examples. Although I have managed to gather a collection of contemporary stories, most of my informants' recollections of the porch come from what I refer to as its "heyday"—from the turn of the twentieth century to the late 1960s and early 1970s. I have organized the stories thematically rather than historically, though I have made a substantial effort to contextualize each story and to address differences that emerge because of the cultural and geographical circumstances.

Because my fieldwork has been limited primarily to Louisiana and Mississippi, I have not drawn firm conclusions about how porch practices in the Deep South might differ from, for example, practices along the East Coast. That is another project. Indeed, I in no way want to claim that this work is the final word on the porch, and I will welcome future studies that fill in gaps here. At the moment, I will venture to say that the undertaking of such a project would undoubtedly reveal differences among the cultures of the "many Souths." At the most fundamental level, different occupations will lead to varied porch practices: one person's shelling of peas will be another person's canning of local fruit. The climate will necessarily affect the level of activity: the relatively cooler porches of coastal South Carolina may invite more enthusiastic, animated uses than those along the sweltering Gulf Coast. The surrounding culture will also orchestrate the stories that get told: one person's "Brer Rabbit" may be another person's "Buki and Lapin."

More significantly, a region's demographics can affect the way a porch is used. The heavily creolized city of New Orleans, with its historical presence of free people of color and a solid black middle class, will necessarily make for more complicated uses in terms of race and class. While traditional boundaries in the South have limited how black people use the front porches of whites, it is not impossible to imagine a middle-class, "old New Orleans" African American limiting the uses of his or her own porch by, say, lower-class whites or even darker-skinned blacks. Or when we imagine the close-knit, working-class homes of mostly white Appalachia, we can wonder how a white outsider might be received. Lee Smith's wonderfully satirical portrayal of the bourgeois Jennifer Bingham in Oral History begins to offer a clue.

In her novel, Smith presents a white ethnic drama of telling and listening in the fictional Hoot Owl Holler, the Appalachian community in which Oral History is set. Jennifer Bingham, a modern-day descendant of the Cantrell family still in Hoot Owl Holler, returns to the community to complete a folklore project. But she fully misses the point of her journey home. She spends an afternoon with her distant family because she has overheard her stepmother deriding the Cantrells' deeply held belief that a ghost has been occupying their family home.

When her folklore instructor (whom Jennifer ultimately marries) waxes enthusiastic over the possibility of tape-recording a ghost, Jennifer journeys "home" to do her share for folklore and for love. She does earn an "A" on her project, but she ultimately fails to "cross the threshold" of her family history. Jennifer has romanticized her estranged family members as "the salt of the earth," even when they reveal their malevolent side to her. She leaves Hoot Owl Holler particularly disturbed by the cruelty of her Uncle Almarine, who plants an unwelcome goodbye kiss on Jennifer's lips. But she eventually changes the experience "all around in her head" from her comfortable distance, classifying the "crude jokes and animal instincts" as the "other side of the pastoral coin" (290–91).

If the Cantrells are suspicious of middle-class whites who are members, albeit distant, of their own family, one indeed must wonder how African Americans would be received on their porch. Even though every outsider, white or black, is subject to suspicion, the inhabitants of Hoot Owl Holler pointedly note their particular unwillingness to receive blacks in their community: Jink Cantrell, one of the novel's several narrators who has grown up in the Appalachian hills, tells us that "he's seen a nigger once, but not close up" (194). Many of these folk say that they "won't have no niggers in the county after sundown" (195). Given such restrictions, we can only assume that the Cantrells would not welcome blacks onto their porches. This particular porch is not a bridge to outsiders; it is a barrier protecting a closed community of Appalachian insiders who rarely lay eyes on people of another race.

Even my brief speculations here about regional influences can justify approaching the porch as variable, depending on its cultural context. However, as I said in the introduction, although this project recognizes differences among southerners and acknowledges that there are "many Souths," I believe there are cross-cultural porch practices that characterize the South as a whole. The song might be different, but the impulse to sing is similar, whether the inspiration is a porch in Louisiana or one in North Carolina. Thus, throughout this work, I negotiate between practices that respect cultural boundaries and those that cut across them.

One prevailing notion that spans cultural boundaries and characterizes the South as a whole is that the porch, though used less frequently today than in the past, remains integral to a southern identity. Though we routinely sound the death knell of the front porch, it continues to endure—if not always in reality, at least in our memories. The following account written by Frances Stirling of Baton Rouge speaks to the porch's centrality:

> As teenagers, we enjoyed the porch as a gathering place to hang out. . . . Our "teenage gang" grew in number, and we spent many an evening on the porch and front steps singing in harmony—sometimes while strumming our ukuleles. Our songs must have sounded sweet on the soft night air because we received many requests from the neighbors up and down the street. As we got further along in school, our times together were noticeably more meaningful. We knew each other so well, the zany times, puppy love romances, joys and sorrows, successes and failures, we knew each other's parents, we loved each other. The wonderful long evenings could not last forever, and we would be going our separate ways too soon. . . . Of this I am certain, wherever that old gang of mine is today, there is a little place in everyone's heart that is still back on the porch.

Perhaps Stirling understates. I wonder if there is not a *big* "place in everyone's heart that is still back on the porch." If porches are less visible physically, they are nevertheless deeply revered in the collective southern consciousness.

DISAPPEARING PORCHES?

Because the death knell of front porches is often sounded, I should address the supposed "absence" of them in the contemporary South. I herein stipulate that porches do not occupy the crucial position in the South today that they merited before the coming of air-conditioning in the 1960s. Southerners, who own nearly 70 percent of the air conditioners in the United States (U.S. Census, No. 1211), have retreated indoors to laze next to their beloved cooling systems. Indeed, the porch has given way to central air, concrete patios, and backyard decks, or to what we in Louisiana call the "car porch" (which provides shelter for automobiles and crawfish boils). Primarily, porches have given way to what Sue Beckham has called "mean little houses" (87).

Consider the following lines written in a letter to me by Lillie Petit Gallagher of Baton Rouge:

> I was born in a house with a front porch.
> I grew up in country houses with front porches.

I hope to die in a house with a front porch.

At the moment, it's obvious, I'm not ready to die.

I live in a house with no front porch.

I content myself with a lone, large watercolor. A front porch fashioned
   from the fragments of an artist's imagination.

Prominently, this front porch hangs above the fireplace mantel in the
   dining room of my house.

This house, with no front porch.

At times, I look at that picture, wistfully remembering the front porches
   of my youth.

Gallagher speaks to the longing of southerners who occupy, usually because of economic constraints, those "mean little houses" rather than homes that boast expansive galleries. The "lone, large watercolor" can certainly symbolize the nostalgia of a culture that has retreated indoors but that continues to grant the porch a central place in its culture. Indeed, the presence of a porch in Gallagher's life is powerful enough to stave off death—she hopes.

One of the informants for this book, Michael Cavanaugh, spent some time during our interview in Baton Rouge theorizing about the "disappearance" of southern porches. Cavanaugh practiced law for many years but retired early to become an independent scholar and writer. His own full-front and full-back porches signify his upper-middle- to upper-class status. His front porch is elegant and inviting. It is the back porch, however, where he and his wife do their daily living and socializing and where Cavanaugh and I held our interview. Giving view to sculptured gardens, including a goldfish pond, and featuring a wooden swing and ceiling fans, the Cavanaughs' back porch is idyllic. It is a frequent site for summer suppers with friends and even for parties. But when we talked about why he does little socializing on his front porch, Cavanaugh replied:

I don't know what kind of psychological dynamics are at play, but I want more anonymity than to sit on my front porch. Now my daddy didn't. Maybe as a preacher he was just a more social person than I am, and as an independent scholar I'm more of a hermit. But why is that true? I guess it's because maybe in the country other people were at a premium, and for me other people can sometimes be kind of a pain. If you're making some sort of hypothesis, you could hypothesize that at the same time that there became so many people per

Michael and Carolyn Cavanaugh's book discussion group on their back porch, Baton Rouge, La., 1999. (Photograph by Jon Griffin Donlon)

square mile, people quit using front porches. Presumably they started using back porches because you still want the benefit of a porch, but you don't want the disadvantages.

Cavanaugh admits in his hypothesis that the front porch's sociability can be a disadvantage for people seeking privacy, and since Americans — perhaps because of contemporary work schedules outside the home, perhaps because of fear of crime, perhaps because of television and air-conditioning—seem to have become more private, the front porch, in particular, has felt the consequences.

Certainly American lifestyles have changed in the last thirty years. Traditional divisions of labor, in which women worked at home and men worked outside the home, have altered so that nearly 60 percent of women now work away from home and, by necessity, away from the porch (U.S. Census, No. 646). The South is less agrarian today, so that snapping home-grown beans on the front porch has been replaced by tearing open a bag of frozen vegetables or, for the lucky, a trip to the local farmers' market. In two-parent families, American fathers are not as free (I like to believe) to relax on the porch after their workday while their wives fix them coffee. There is, typically, more sharing of domestic tasks, calling for fathers to spend more time indoors with the family.

Our perceptions of crime have undoubtedly been a factor in the porch's decline. One informant, an older woman in Baton Rouge, told me that she "jokingly" calls her porch, situated in a neighborhood with a relatively high crime rate, "shoot city" because she can sit and "watch bullets go by" (Unnamed, Oct. 18, 1996). And a schoolteacher in New Orleans told me that she and her mother are afraid to sit out on the porch for fear of crime (Unnamed, July 19, 1996). Americans, apparently more fearful of crime, retreat indoors to activate security systems, if they own them.

Most often discussed, though, are the effects of air-conditioning — beloved, cherished, never-to-be-taken-for-granted, never-to-be-undervalued, blessed air-conditioning. As southern historian Raymond Arsenault writes:

> Ask any Southerner over thirty years of age to explain why the South has changed in recent decades, and he may begin with the civil rights movement or industrialization. But sooner or later he will come around to the subject of air conditioning. For better or worse, he will tell you, the air conditioner has changed the nature of Southern life. Some Southerners will praise air conditioning and wonder out loud how they ever lived without it. Others will argue that the South is going to hell, not in a hand basket, but in an air-conditioned Chevy. (598)

Hot weather is so central to a southern consciousness that Ulrich Bonnell Phillips opens his 1929 classic, *Life and Labor in the Old South*, with the line, "Let us begin by discussing the weather, for that has been the chief agency in making the South distinctive." He continues by claiming that the hot, miserable southern climate "fostered the cultivation of the staple crops, which promoted the plantation system, which brought the importation of Negroes, which not only gave rise to chattel slavery but created a lasting race problem" (3). Obviously, Phillips oversimplifies the institution of slavery in the southern United States, but he does indicate how central the unbearable heat was for southerners before the days of air-conditioning, which, by the 1950s, had taken firm hold on the region. By 1955, one of every twenty-two American homes had some form of air-conditioning, but in the South the figure was closer to one of every ten. In 1960, over 400,000 southern homes had central units. And during the early 1970s, millions of southern homes had air-conditioning installed for the first time. By the seventies, as Arsenault puts it, "The age of the push-button 'climate-conditioned' home had arrived" (597–611).

In the push-button era, the porch has necessarily become less central to southerners' everyday lives. I confess that I myself make little use of my porch during July and August, unbearable months in Louisiana. The 100°F temperatures and the 100 percent humidity are hard to suffer when a push-button, icy-cool world awaits inside. And, of course, that icy-cool world includes a television. With each American watching about one thousand hours of television every year, the porch will necessarily feel the withdrawal of families indoors (U.S. Census, No. 914).

Admittedly, then, the porch has decreased in popularity over the last thirty years. However, it has not altogether "disappeared." Often, prevalent middle-class notions of culture motivate lamentations over the porch's demise. A drive, however, through working-class neighborhoods where porches are still used because homes may not have air-conditioning, and even past upper-class estates where freshly painted porticos front neoclassical estates solely for decorative purposes, reveals that porches are still very much a part of the southern architectural landscape. Porches have disappeared largely from middle-class ranch-style homes, but not from the South altogether. Consider, for example, the following statement by my former student, Kenyada Corley. A young African American woman from New Orleans, Kenyada was enrolled in my Introduction to Folklore course at LSU in 1997. During a unit on vernacular architecture, as we were discussing the role of the porch, the rest of the students (middle-class whites) began to lament the disappearance of the front porch. Kenyada, the only black student in the class, sat silent. She later told me in an interview, "Every house I lived in had a porch. They even had a balcony. I remember our class discussion about how porches had 'disappeared,' and I was thinking, 'Where have they gone?'"

Of course, in the city of New Orleans—birthplace of the American shotgun house—they haven't gone anywhere. As I have already mentioned, some high-crime neighborhoods have driven people inside for safety. And New Orleanians, like other Louisianans, love their air-conditioning. But the front porch is by no means dead in the city. And even in middle-class, suburban homes, the porch is making something of a comeback, as illustrated by Algonquin's highly success-ful book, *Out on a Porch*, and its accompanying annual calendar.

I believe—and the enthusiasm of my informants in this project confirms—that many southerners still consider themselves porch people, even if for the last twenty to thirty years we have often found the kitchen table a more com-fortable venue in which to carry out erstwhile porch practices. Southern porches have been and will continue to be vital settings for the construction of cultural identity.

"PLACES" AND "SPACES"

In my interviews with people, I have explored how porches have contributed to the construction of a southern identity within—and between—specific folk groups. Some useful definitions have shaped this exploration, in particular the definitions of "place" and "space" established by Michel de Certeau in *The Prac-tice of Everyday Life*. In this book, de Certeau defines "place" as an established "configuration of positions" that has been dictated by the dominant culture; "space," on the other hand, is "composed of intersections of mobile elements." In other words, "place" is an area controlled by the prevailing culture. Indi-viduals, however, can resist societal regulations by manipulating a controlled "place," thereby recasting it as a creatively used "space." "Space" is thus "prac-ticed place" (117). My project turns on de Certeau's definitions to examine how the porch—a "place" that is liminally situated between public and private spheres—has served also as a "space" where southerners can forge an identity within and between designated folk groups.

I find de Certeau's definitions more useful than arbitrary because they indi-cate how the porch is a site where people can either gain or lose power. Thus, when I use "place" in quotation marks throughout this book, I mean that the porch is governed by certain constraints, be they constraints of family, commu-nity, gender, class, race, sexuality, politics, or even housing regulations. I use "space," again in quotation marks, to signify that individuals can gain power for themselves by reshaping a "place" in their own terms—hence this book's title: *Swinging in Place: Porch Life in Southern Culture*. The word "swinging" captures the liminality of the porch—the modulating between spheres yet resting in neither. This negotiation of public and private boundaries occurs in a "place" largely controlled by others. We are, however, free, to a certain extent, to create a unique, living "space" for ourselves. My main purpose, then, is to explore how southerners have orchestrated porch life to seize and display power.

I have taken an interdisciplinary approach to this subject matter, in that I am situating the work within the fields of folklore, vernacular architecture, cultural history, and literary studies. The interrogation of the porch includes a diverse group of people both inside and outside the academy, and embraces both theoretical and practical concerns. Indeed, as I discuss in the conclusion, recent work in urban studies calls for the construction of porches in new neighborhoods, not only to facilitate a sense of community, but also to provide a place for privacy. Because I take an interdisciplinary approach, my method is somewhat unusual within academic studies in that it places personal narratives in dialogue with literary ones, thereby narrowing the gap between the everyday and the literary.

PORCH "SPACES" IN SOUTHERN LITERATURE

Porch power is so integral to southern culture that much of southern literature has used the porch to symbolize social practices. I have already mentioned the popular book, *Out on a Porch*. To accompany its glossy photographs, this book includes numerous excerpts from southern literature that depict the life of the porch. More recently, folklorist Trudier Harris has contributed *The Power of the Porch: The Storyteller's Craft in Zora Neale Hurston, Gloria Naylor, and Randall Kenan*. Harris's purpose is different from mine here. In her published series of lectures, Harris uses the porch as a metaphor for oral storytelling. She is interested in the orality of southern African American writers who construct novels as though they are porch storytellers for porch listeners. Harris reminds us that the porch is a powerful metaphor for the storytelling, community, and socializing that have shaped much of southern literature. Because of the power of the porch in southern literature, I include significant literary examples in this discussion. But I want to explain in more detail my rationale for using both real-life and fictionalized narratives to illustrate southern porch culture.

As I mentioned earlier in this chapter, a strong motivation for including literary narratives is to broaden significantly our discussion of porch culture in terms of region. My face-to-face fieldwork has been limited to southern Louisiana; thus, providing examples from novels set in other parts of the South increases the representation of different cultures. In addition, a fictional narrator's anonymity in a literary work is useful, as is the aesthetic distance created between the writer and the reader: A fictional narrative can offer stories that real people may be hesitant to tell a folklorist face to face or to document in a letter.

Looking at real and literary texts together also reveals the dynamic relationship between folklore and literature. Folklorists tend to champion everyday, oral traditions; literary scholars analyze written narratives—often, the more complicated the better. But, as Trudier Harris's metaphor of "the power of the porch" indicates, southern literature itself rests in everyday oral practices; thus the edges between "oral" and "written" can get rather fuzzy. Indeed, William Faulkner, in his second introduction to *The Sound and the Fury*, claims that southerners "have never got and probably will never get, anywhere with music or the plastic forms." Instead, he declares, "We need to talk, to tell, since oratory is our heritage" (413). His famous assertion affirms the link between southern literature and its grounding in oral, everyday culture.

Folklorist Linda Dégh has said, "Folklore is the product of an ongoing historical process that consolidates the interaction of literary and oral, professional and nonprofessional, formal and informal, constructed and improvised creativity" (1). Granted, Dégh's focus is on the relationship between mass media and folklore, but her point remains relevant. Our everyday, oral narratives illustrate that the porch is a folk institution integral to our ordinary lives. By showing how southern fiction has constructed the porch as a literary device, we bring life and literature closer together.

This chapter has established that the porch is a transitional "space" on which individuals, if they are able to seize power, can create an identity. But understanding how individuals create an identity means identifying the norms of a culture that influence an individual's behavior. In Chapter 2, "Living the Everyday Life," I focus on southern norms, generalizing that a "southern" identity is grounded in commitment to community and family. I then show how porches—front and back—are used to regulate the interaction between family and community. In particular, front porches function as a public stage on which the rules of southern decorum are enforced, whereas back porches are workplaces tucked out of view so that social rules can be relaxed. How families make use of these different spaces is an indicator of what kind of impression they want to communicate to others.

Although southern identity is about family and community, it nevertheless is often entangled in contests of race, gender, class, and sexuality. Chapter 3, "Setting Boundaries of Race and Class," begins by reviewing this complicated architectural history, tracing how the porch is a creolized structure, historically rooted in African, West Indian, and European forms. Talk of hybridity, particularly racial hybridity, inevitably leads to discussions of "boundary maintenance." To advance such conversations, Chapter 3 looks more closely at the porch relationship of blacks and whites in the South.

The policing of boundaries is not limited to race, however. As William Faulkner's *Absalom, Absalom!* shows, such boundary maintenance on southern porches usually involves the interplay of race and class. When a slave bars Sutpen, a "white trash" boy, from the door of a rich, white plantation owner, Sutpen learns about intraracial boundaries of class. Porches can be "places" where those who possess the right combination of money, power, and privilege can assert control by admitting some and excluding others.

The porch may be framed by the norms of a society, but Chapter 4, "Shaping the Family," shows how it is also an arena wherein families work out everyday relationships of power. Informants have remembered, from their childhoods, generational conflicts in which their parents confined them to the porch for safety or even for punishment. Informants have also talked about how men and women within families have used the porch differently. In its heyday before the 1970s, the porch traditionally belonged to women during the day but to fathers after work, when they expected to enjoy their leisure time on the front porch while their wives prepared dinner. Thus, the public world of men could overpower the domestic sphere of women.

Not every family with a porch, however, is necessarily functional. Some people have confided to me that they used porches to escape domestic oppression. Dorothy Allison's provocative novel *Bastard Out of Carolina* shows, for example, how the porch is a semipublic "space" of safety that enables a young girl to escape her stepfather's sexual abuse.

The discussion of family dynamics in Chapter 4 leads logically to an examination of courtship and romance in Chapter 5, "Fanning the Flames." Because the porch is a liminal space, somewhere between public and private, it responds to the outside constraints of the community as well as to the demands of the home. Few porch activities demonstrate the demands of porch liminality better than courtship and romance rituals. Tradition tells us that the porch is a safe, semipublic site for heterosexual romances to bloom: It is private enough for the intimate whisperings of a young man and woman, but it is also public enough for parents to believe that no inappropriate hanky-panky will occur.

Such established traditions of porch romance typically celebrate the nuclear, middle- to upper-class family. And indeed, Chapter 5 recounts many such celebratory traditional stories. But from this traditional context I turn to courtship stories from the "other" side of the porch, including stories from gays and lesbians who use the porch to create a "space" in which to assert their sexual identities.

In this book as a whole, I want to show how the porch is much more than a mere shady transition for sipping iced tea—though it certainly is that. It is a powerfully charged "space" that has long been integral to the everyday lives of southerners and has produced—and been produced by—norms of southern culture. The following chapter takes a closer look at these cultural norms associated with the porch.

Although the porch is framed in contests of power, it nevertheless is a commonplace arena where families perform chores, raise children, rehash community gossip, escape each other, and strive to verify a sense of belonging. In many of these customary activities, power struggles are not consciously undertaken. For the moment, I want to consider this routine, everyday porch life by allowing several informants to speak for themselves. I have intentionally decontextualized the following stories, with one exception: All of them depict porches of decades past. But while the stories are pre-1980s, the specific time period is often ambiguous. In addition, the towns or cities in these stories could be located most anywhere in the South. I am decontextualizing the informants' accounts to this extent precisely because I want to celebrate the traditional life of the porch, which cuts across cultural and regional boundaries. Although I certainly remain suspicious of nostalgia throughout much of this work, admittedly I am recognizing it here. Taken together, the different stories below offer an array of life experiences fitting for many southerners who are lucky enough to have had—or to still have—a porch or two or, for the truly lucky, three:

It was in our porch swing that I did most of my reading. And then, of course, there was the courting carried on under the soft moonlight of a summer night. Little girls played jacks on front galleries, and boys and girls played cards and checkers. In the glow of the streetlight at night, the older girls told hair-raising ghost stories to squealing little ones as they huddled on the front steps. Ladies sat in porch rockers and cooled themselves with fans.
—Emma H. Major

We would sit on the porch of my grandmother's large house, all afternoon and evening after supper. She would tell us about when she was a little girl. We

Mountain child shooting a slingshot from the porch of his home near Buckhorn, Kentucky. (Photograph by Marion Post Wolcott, 1940; Library of Congress Prints and Photographs Division [LC-USF33-031095-M4])

would cut up okra, shell peas, string beans, peel peaches and pears—all of this for canning. She did her quilting and sewing, just about everything from this front porch.
—Theresa Haydel Griffith

Our six-foot square porch was nestled in the "L" of the frame house. A swing, hanging on the right side of the porch, faced a windowless wall. A perfect movie screen. My two sisters and I would sit in the swing and wait for the show. When we heard a car approaching, one of us would dash across the

Millworker's children eating watermelon on porch of rented house six miles north of Roxboro, North Carolina. (Photograph by Dorothea Lange, 1939; Library of Congress Prints and Photographs Division [LC-USF34-020141-E])

yard, climb upon the old tree stump behind the swing, and do crazy gyrations. The headlights from the car projected the image of the stump and person upon the wall. As the car moved closer and passed the house, the shadow on the wall seemed to come alive, move across the screen, and then fade away. What fun!!

—Frances Lithgoe

Living the Everyday Life

Frances Wood Lithgoe (seated on left), aged ten years, with sisters Jane (on right) and Sue (standing), Henderson, Ky. (Photograph by Mrs. Owen Wood [mother], 1934)

When my first two boys were half-grown, we had a Hawaiian Luau. And we made it a family reunion inviting people from far and near. . . . Hubby had obtained some long boards about fourteen inches wide. He put them down on the porch floor and placed ten inches of bricks on the ends and in the middle. Then all the pillows were put down on both sides of the board. This enabled us to seat about twenty people, young and old. Only one eighty-year-old sat in a rocker. Everything else had been removed from the porch. We covered the board with cloths and then put the utensils and plates down. Centerpieces were pineapples to be eaten later. The decorations and lei necklaces made it very festive.
—Vivien E. Markwith

During the summer months, my parents and I spent lots of time rocking and watching the world ride by. I first became aware of the different makes of cars as Daddy pointed them out to me. I remember seeing a small English Austin, a Hudson Terraplane, and a silvery-grey Chrysler with the stream-

lined look.. I remember, too, the Greyhound buses that passed several times
a day.
—Frankie Platte

Returning from dancing very late at night, we'd walk quietly on the steps to sit
for a moment on the swing, maybe a good night kiss, and, lo and behold,
Mama would snap on the gallery light, which was the signal for "Come In!"
—Elida Caillouet

Whenever we were young, my family and I sang together. We would sit in the
evening or at night, and we would all sing—Mama and Daddy and the girls,
not the boys. Johnnie was tenor, Margie was alto, and I'd just sing whatever—I was born in the middle! We would sing gospel. Aunt Queenie, she
was a Pentecost, she would teach us a few chords on the guitar. The people
over at the Pentecostal church, who were *way* across the countryside, could
hear us sing. We *really* sang. Oh Daddy loved to sing. . . . When I was growing up, if people were gone somewhere, they would take the chairs that
were out on the front porch and they'd turn them around and lean them up
against the wall. So if you went to a house and the chair was turned around
backwards and leaning up against the wall, there was nobody home.
—Nell Coleman

Sometimes in order to enjoy our porch on summer nights, it was necessary to
burn a "mosquito pot." The smoke kept the bugs and other pests away. I
can still smell the burning of the coals. . . . Then there were the warm nights
when a group of my male friends would gather on our porch to harmonize.
How beautiful their strong young voices sounded when singing "We Were
Sailing Along on Moonlight Bay," "Sweet Adeline," or "Carolina Moon."
They were good boys and good singers, and those were the "good old days."
—Grace Piner Boshamer

On Sundays, you had to get up to go to church—you had to go to Sunday
School, then you'd go home, and you'd eat dinner around 12:00. Then you'd
go back to church. And when you'd come from church, everybody would
migrate to the front porch, and you'd have dessert. The whole family—little

"Mother's Front Porch." Home of Marguerite Whetstone, Winston-Salem, N.C.
(Photograph by Becky Shank, 1990)

children, adults, everybody—spent time on the front porch. On Saturday
evenings, my grandmother would go in her garden for Sunday morning, and
she would shell peas on her front porch. She would clean and cut her okra.
Sometimes we had to go in and take a bath, and we had to change clothes.
And then you'd visit from porch to porch. That was an everyday thing, not
just a Sunday thing, particularly in the summer.
—Crystal Jones

On any given Sunday, [Mother's front porch] will hold an assortment of moms
and dads, grandparents, cousins, aunts, uncles, and toddlers, some of
whom will stretch out on the steps or haul out kitchen chairs and crowd in.
Several conversations usually go on at once, but anyone accustomed to such
can keep up with all that is being said. I remember how my grandfather,
Pop, would ease himself into a rocker, hang his cane on the arm of the chair,
and make joking comments to everyone.
—Rebecca Gentry Shank

After a day in the cotton field, we would drag to the house, dog-tired, with sweat pouring down our face. Mother would have supper almost ready. We would pull off our field clothes—she insisted that we were covered from the sun—bonnets, long sleeved shirts, blue jeans, shoes and socks, and gloves. I can remember how good it felt when the slight breeze first hit me after I had stripped to my underwear on the back porch. . . . After baths and dinner, we would all go out on the front porch and listen to stories of when Mother and Daddy were growing up. They told about how they had to work twice as hard when they were growing up as we did. . . . Lots of social news was gathered from that porch.
—C. Jean Jackson

We sat on the porch to catch a faint breeze, if possible, shelled peas and ate watermelon. My cousins and my friends and I played there, even when it was raining—one of the best spots to be during a shower—you could hear and smell the rain. At night we would watch bats fly around the light pole across the street and fire flies twinkling. We knew all of the people living within a few blocks of us. It gave me . . . cozy, secure feelings to know, see, and listen to so many grown-ups.
—Vee Taylor

The front porch, lined with rickety rocking chairs, was a neighborhood gathering place for coffee drinking and local gossip. My parents knew the schedule of all working people in the neighborhood. These people worked in different places on Front Street and walked past our house on their way to and from work and would bring news of happenings occurring in town during the work day. Among those passing was a pair of deaf brothers who were twins and lived in the next block. Although my parents did not know how to sign, they could communicate with them and understand exactly the stories they were telling.
—Mattie Lou Faroldo Furby

From these enduring memories, we hear of the daily chores of "cutting up okra," "peeling pears," or "quilting and sewing." We hear of soft nights where lovers

Living the Everyday Life

steal kisses before "Mama snaps the light on." We are told of children playing jacks and cards, of moms and dads and siblings and neighbors telling stories—true or invented, or both—of community members keeping tabs on each other. New models of cars get noticed and even incorporated into porch games. Families sing their favorite songs so enthusiastically that the "people over at the Pentecostal church, who were *way* across the countryside, could hear." One teller recalls "good singers," "good boys," and "the good old days." The community is so secure that families can advertise their being out of town by turning porch chairs to face the house wall. Small wonder that porches can make us nostalgic! Most of us today, at the very least, put our mail on hold, stop the delivery of the newspaper, and place several lights on timers in order to give our homes a lived-in look while we are away. We certainly do not advertise our being gone.

But nostalgia for a life that seems to have slipped away is not enough reason to read and celebrate these memories. From these stories, we can draw several important conclusions about the larger social and psychological significance of charmed porch "spaces" in southern culture.

PORCH ETHOS

Taken together, the above stories reveal a characteristic spirit—an ethos—of community and family that characterizes the South as a whole. One social activity that binds many different southerners together is the general affection for sharing conversation. Southerners *need* to tell stories to enthusiastic listeners. In the words of the poet Allen Tate, "The Southerner always talks to somebody else, and this somebody else, after varying intervals, is given his turn." Typically, according to Tate, southern talk "is not going anywhere; it is not about anything. It is *about the people who are talking*, even if they never refer to themselves" [italics in original] (584). Such community-oriented conversation is, of course, not limited to southerners, but it is a mode frequently used in the South to establish connections in a shared society.

Southerners of all stripes have customarily taken pride in their skill with the spoken word, an enthusiasm that has led to the development of one of the richest oral cultures in the world. In addition to the Native American tradition that existed in the South before the arrival of Europeans, the region has inherited strong storytelling legacies from such source areas as Ireland, West Africa, and southern England, and these have been reinforced by the physical isolation of agrarian settlements and by a conservative mentality that privileges ancestral ways (Burrison 2).

Zora Neale Hurston, in celebrating her own African American oral culture, characterizes these exceptional verbal skills of people in the South. In her autobiography, *Dust Tracks on a Road*, she explains how the "average Southern child, white or black, is raised on simile and invective," and she says:

> It is an everyday affair to hear somebody called a mullet-headed, mule-eared, wall-eyed, hog-nosed, 'gator-faced, shad-mouthed, screw-necked, goat-bellied, puzzle-gutted, camel-backed, butt-sprung, battle-hammed, knock-kneed, razor-legged, box-ankled, shovel-footed, unmated so-and-so! . . . [Southerners] can tell you in simile exactly how you walk and smell. They can furnish a picture gallery of your ancestors, and a notion of what your children will be like. (135–36)

Hurston affirms southerners' appetite for orality, noting how they take "their comparisons right out of the barnyard and the woods," being, overall, "not given to book-reading" (136). Many southerners have used their talents to conserve a wide variety of storytelling genres and, in so doing, have sustained a cultural system in which talking is an individual's primary means of social interaction. The porch, because it stands ready to receive others, is an ideal space for southern storytellers to find enthusiastic listeners.

Kate Daniels, in her essay "Porch-Sitting and Southern Poetry," speaks to this relationship between porches and storytelling. Discussing the narrative impulse that characterizes much of southern poetry, Daniels recalls her paternal grandmother's porch in Richmond, Virginia:

> In spite of the pronounced absence of literature, stories lived all around my grandmother—if not in the pages of books, then in the tales she told of our family; of her early life on a farm in Tidewater Virginia; of the peddlers and salesmen who regularly rapped on the porch steps before venturing up them; of the conditions of life during the depression, which remained vivid in her mind; and, of course, the neighbors. . . . On every porch, stories *lived*, and occasionally, when a neighbor would walk up the broad stairs onto our porch,

or we would cross the street to one of theirs, I don't recall anything beyond the most preliminary of polite conversation before the stories would begin. (62–63)

Daniels's porch memories, as well as those that opened this chapter, certainly portray the porch as a celebrated site of storytelling, representing oral genres from traditional folk stories to unique personal experience stories. We have heard of "older girls" telling "hair-raising ghost stories to squealing little ones," of children going "out on the front porch" in order to "listen to stories of when Mother and Daddy were growing up," of passersby who would "stop for a short chat," and even of adults who worked hard to "understand exactly the stories" told to them by deaf twins who passed by.

It is largely because of continuing agrarian traditions and values that storytelling has continued to thrive. Though much of the contemporary South is industrialized, it has become that way only slowly. The above stories testify to the southern legacy of agrarianism. Adults and children would, on their porches, "cut up okra, shell peas, string beans, peel peaches and pears—all of this for canning." Or children, "after a day in the cotton field," would "drag to the house, dog tired, with sweat pouring down [their] face[s]." Nearly every informant I talked with or received letters from had some memory of performing daily "farm chores" on the porch, the most remembered being the task of "shelling peas"—crowder peas, black-eyed peas, or field peas, all of which would inevitably be served with an iron-skillet pan of cornbread. The stories reveal typical crops cultivated in the agrarian South—peas, cotton, peaches—and, although the crops might vary from region to region, the stories show how the everyday management of these crops has brought families together on different porches throughout the South as a whole.

Because the South was, during the reign of the porch, predominantly an agrarian culture, families not only grew their own food, but also created their own leisure—much of it on the porch. Storytelling was, and still is, a primary form of leisure. In the oppressive heat of the South, particularly the Deep South, it is often hard to muster the energy to move more than lips and arms for conversation. But we also see in the above stories how children have used the porch to play the traditional games of jacks, cards, and checkers, and they have also invented games, as illustrated by the story of the sisters who used the auto-

Porch of African American tenant house, showing household equipment,
Person County, N.C. (Photograph by Dorothea Lange, 1939; Library of Congress
Prints and Photographs Division [LC-USF34-020128-E])

mobile headlights to cast a shadow play on the "windowless wall." Vivien E.
Markwith's family even used its Virginia porch to create a Hawaiian luau for the
children.

The view from the porch indeed sheds light on the changing culture of the
mid-twentieth century. The subject of "automobiles" appears more than once—
from children using them to facilitate their games to their learning of the "En-

glish Austin," the "Hudson Terraplane," and the "silvery-grey Chrysler with the stream-lined look." As the South developed from a pedestrian culture to an automobile culture, so did the porch. Perhaps fewer walkers stopped in to chat, but a new activity was created—listening for cars, identifying them, and using them to strengthen a family's leisure time. (We are reminded here of how Rose Anne St. Romain's grandmother put on fresh makeup before she went out to wave to people in their automobiles, whether she knew them or not.) The ethos of the South encourages family members and neighbors to gather together to work, talk, watch, sing, play games, and visit with others. And because the porch is a liminal space, families necessarily intersect with the community as they live out their everyday lives. Families and neighbors seem to know each other in these stories; as a result, people can advertise leaving their houses by turning their porch chairs against the wall, and children can have "cozy, secure feelings to know, see, and listen to so many grown-ups."

Because of the ongoing negotiation between family and community, between self and other, southern identities have historically been about more than rugged individualism. A history of front porches means a history of others sitting, watching, evaluating, and shaping public behavior. Thus, the porch has contributed to a kind of instability of identity for many southerners, by breaking down boundaries between inner and outer worlds. On the porch, one's sense of self cannot be separated from the perception of external expectations—from the norms of the community. And if the expectations become overwhelming, they can be destructive to a person's identity.

This pervasive awareness of others' expectations, on the liminal space of the porch, has created the need for what Erving Goffman, in The Presentation of Self in Everyday Life, calls "impression management." Goffman says:

Sometimes the individual will act in a thoroughly calculating manner, expressing himself in a given way solely in order to give the kind of impression to others that is likely to evoke from them a specific response he is concerned to obtain. Sometimes the individual will be calculating in his activity but be relatively unaware that this is the case. Sometimes he will intentionally and consciously express himself in a particular way, but chiefly because the tradition[s] of his group or social status require this kind of expression. . . . Sometimes the traditions of an individual's role will lead him to give a well-designed impression of a particular kind and yet he may be neither consciously nor unconsciously disposed to create such an impression. (6)

In short, Goffman is saying that we might be conscious or unconscious of our techniques of "impression management." Moreover, we might be engaging in such techniques either to meet our own needs or because tradition demands it. In other words, the very techniques for impression management are in response to an individual's continual negotiation with the cultural norms of a larger community.

Certainly the front porch is an ideal stage for defining the impressions that we want to convey. We have already heard about how people will put on fresh clothes, women will apply fresh lipstick, and "ladies" will cool themselves with fans while sitting on the front porch. The techniques for controlling one's image are often used in everyday, unconscious ways simply because tradition insists on it. But while the front porch, in particular, is largely about managing impressions, it is not always about displaying one's best self. One of the storytellers at the beginning of this chapter talked about how her grandmother did "everything" on her front porch, from quilting to sewing to stringing beans. The unlimited use of the front porch in these and other examples is obviously connected to class: It is a functional response to not having a back porch. Not every small, working-class home is graced with a back porch large enough for work.

For the moment, though, I will focus on those houses that do have both a front and a back porch. Remember from Chapter 1 that Frenchy Hodges said the front porch is a "breast-pocket / of a family's up-and-coming-ness / Or down-and-outed-ness." Later in the same poem, Hodges talks about the difference between a front porch and a back porch:

> Back porches
> Were for resting things
> Like muddy shoes
> Sweaty shirts
> Just-killed squirrels,
> Rabbits, 'coons or 'possums. . . .
>
> Back porches
> Were for resting things.

Living the Everyday Life

Hodges's back porch is more about working, seeking privacy, and hiding unsightly items than it is about being a showplace. How a family makes different uses of front and back porches says much about its techniques of impression management—about how it controls the image it wants to present to others in the community. This, in turn, says much about how people must negotiate an individual identity in relation to community norms.

Goffman again usefully differentiates between what he calls "front regions" and "back regions." The term "front region" refers to the area where a performance actually takes place. As Goffman says, "The performance of an individual in a front region may be seen as an effort to give the appearance that his activity in the region maintains and embodies certain standards" (107). These "standards" fall into two groupings for Goffman: standards of "politeness," which he defines as "talk" or "gestures"; and standards of "decorum," which have to do with "the way in which the performer comports himself while in visual or aural range of the audience but not necessarily engaged in talk with them" (107).

In contrast to the front region is the "back region," which is "a place, relative to a given performance, where the impression fostered by the performance is knowingly contradicted as a matter of course" (112). In the back region, the "tools" and "props" for the front region are hidden. Goffman's clearest example of the difference between a front and back region is the funeral home, where the family is discouraged from seeing—or even forbidden to see—the area in the back where the body of its loved one is prepared for viewing in the front room. The back region is thus subject to more control.

Obviously, Goffman is talking about more than a literal performance with literal props. He is talking about everyday human performances, in which we discriminate between what we willingly display for others and what we want to keep hidden. As they negotiate the norms of family and community, southern families have used their front and back porch-regions to control that which is freely displayed and that which is tucked out of view.

A DAY IN THE LIFE OF THE PORCH

Leah Beth Simpson, of Amite, Louisiana, offers in the following account, set in the Great Depression, a detailed description of how her grandmother used her front and back porches throughout the day, controlling the impressions that she wanted to convey to others:

I have such fond memories of my own grandmother and her front and back porches. My grandmother, Mrs. Emma Lee Houeye, lived on what is now Highway 51, downtown in Amite, Louisiana, in the home she and her husband built in 1904. Of course, at the time the house was built, Highway 51 was a dirt road with dirt paths along its side for pedestrians to walk to and from the heart of town. The house had a wide front porch all the way across the front of the house and a back porch along the side of the kitchen and dining room.

In the morning hours (before dinner, which was the 12 o'clock meal; supper was the night meal), my grandmother sat in a rocking chair on the back porch and prepared vegetables for dinner (she took in boarders and fed all five of her grandchildren every day of their school years). She received visitors on the back porch, and many times they pitched in and helped shuck corn, hull peas, or pare potatoes while they visited.

After dinner, my grandmother took a bath, dusted herself generously with very white lilac bath powder, put on her bathrobe and took a nap, after which she dressed in her Sunday go-to-meeting dress, took her Palmetto fan (in summer) and sat in the rocking chair on the front porch, where she received visitors and chatted with the "passer byers" out on the sidewalk.

In this caring, nostalgic account of life at her grandmother's house, Leah Beth Simpson portrays South Louisiana culture at a time when the porch was vital to a family and a community. Houeye took in boarders during the Depression years, and because, in this account, the porch is so closely tied to subsistence activities to keep the family going (remember, she fed her five grandchildren every day), it is intimately tied to work activities — particularly the back porch. If neighbors stop by for a spontaneous visit, they pitch in and help "shuck corn, hull peas, or pare potatoes." The rules of socializing must be negotiated with the necessity for work, the necessity for a family's survival.

Porch dwellers can, indeed, put out two signals: one for work, one for leisure. When visitors arrive during work periods, these worlds of labor and leisure intersect. But unlike Goffman's "back region," where people are usually forbidden to see the tools and props used in the "front region," the back porch is not totally hidden from view. Community visitors are welcome to climb the steps to the back porch (indeed, in the next chapter, we'll see how some people are even *consigned*

Living the Everyday Life

to it), if they are willing to suspend the requirement of "porch as community showplace" and to accept the back porch as a family work station.

Houeye's front porch, however, is in every way a showplace. It is strictly for "receiving" and "chatting," a place to connect with the social life of the community. The front porch is conspicuous in its owner's leisure pursuits, complete with Houeye in a "Sunday go-to-meeting dress," a "Palmetto fan (in summer)," and a "rocking chair" in which Houeye sat to receive passersby. Even during the economic hardships of the Great Depression, Simpson says, her grandmother, though forced to take in boarders to survive, "carried on the tradition of the 'lady of the house.'" She used her porch to demonstrate to the community that the Depression had not gotten the best of her, that she remembered a time when her large house was not a boardinghouse. The fact that the grandmother could sit on her front porch purely for leisure during the Depression is indicative of some degree of class privilege not available to everyone in the South.

Today, Leah Beth Simpson lives about a block away from where her grandmother's house once stood on Highway 51 in Amite. Her own home was built in 1897, and her restorations have attempted to keep the integrity of the original house in mind. Simpson, a woman of seemingly tireless energy, not only pursued a long nursing career, but also devoted countless volunteer hours to community and home preservation. She has served for years on the Historic Preservation Commission in Amite. Her commitment to family and community, to labor and leisure, certainly must owe a debt to her grandmother's porch, itself a meeting point for family and community.

Edith Mewborn Martin of Snow Hill, North Carolina, in recalling her childhood home, echoes elements of Leah Beth Simpson's story, but the boundaries are not as neatly drawn. She says:

> The front porch represented fun, recreation, and pleasure in our lives. Even though nearly every evening, there was the minor chore of shelling peas or butter beans, or snapping snap beans to get them ready for the next day's summer feast at the large, oval dining room table . . . compared to all the other work and chores, shelling a few beans was more fun than work! We gathered and sat and talked as we shelled. And after dark, if still not completed, we would move into the house, turn on the tall Philco radio, and listen to "Henry Aldridge."

Home of Leah Beth Simpson, Amite, La. (Photograph by Jon Griffin Donlon, 1999)

Home of Wilson Adrien Petit, grandfather to Lillie Gallagher, Cut Off, La.
(Photograph by Florine Aline Petit, ca. 1928)

Such activities, which were "more fun than work," contrast with the daily chores that took place on Martin's back porch; these, she says, "represented *work*." On this back porch, she and her sisters helped their mother to keep the household going:

> We girls sat out there with our mother, chipping in, to get vegetables and fruits ready for canning. There was a hand pump convenient for washing. Then we peeled and cut up the produce, and made it ready to pack in the jars for their steam-sealing water bath in the big pots on our wooden stove—until REA brought us electricity. . . . The back porch, though screened in, had very little shade from the piercing afternoon sun.

But despite the hard work, there were penetrations of play. They would "sit in a circle getting the fruit and vegetables ready while [their] mama 'would tell stories about her 'old-timey days,' family members, and her good sense advice." Work and leisure, in Edith Martin's account, are bound together on both the front and the back porches.

Lillie Petit Gallagher, who grew up along Bayou Lafourche in South Louisiana during the 1940s, offers an additional account of using front and back porches:

The front porch was as informative as a daily, local newspaper. . . . From the front porch, a lone oyster lugger, iron oyster tongs strapped securely to her wheelhouse, could be seen riding high on the bayou. Her big, broad beam slowly left a wake. She was making her way south, out to the oyster beds in the protected coastal waters of the gulf. It would be several weeks, but in time, back she would come. Sunk low, her deck, piled high with oysters, barely skimmed the waterline. Up the bayou she sailed, to the Cloverly Canal, to Little Lake, through Lake Salvador, to river streets of the French Quarter. The oysters had gone to market. And when the little lugger returned, emptied of her succulent cargo, from the vantage point of the front porch, an entire economic market cycle of a watery harvest had been witnessed. . . .

But not to be forgotten in the scheme of porches was the back porch or 'tween porch, the one sometimes found "between" the kitchen and the main house. These were strictly work porches. No lollygagging allowed on a back or 'tween porch. A specific hierarchy of activity was observed and rigorously practiced. Back porches were serious, open-air work parlors where a different kind of labor took place. Bread could be kneaded and left to rise in a sunny spot two steps away from an old outdoor oven. A spare slab of marble, usually a broken cemetery headstone, was used to clean fish, chickens, rabbits, game and turtles. Placed over a barrel in an open area it could be easily washed down with disinfectant after use. Corn could be shucked, cleaned and desilvered. Mostly it was benches which provided seating on the back porch, but an occasional rocking chair could be found. It was usually reserved for an elderly grandmother or aunt, who, with only a nod or word, kept the back porch going. Loitering children were not encouraged or tolerated.

By contrast, on a front porch packed with gliders, rockers, swings and bounce chairs, peas and butter beans could be shelled and snapped, quilt pieces hand stitched, pillow covers embroidered, decoys whittled, doilies crocheted, ice cream cranked . . . all in addition to the ubiquitous exchange of gossip, politics, storytelling and careful watching of the passing scene.

Lillie Petit Gallagher's marvelous detail bears witness to the cycle of family life, the cycle of a community, indeed the "cycle of a watery harvest" of South Louisiana aquaculture. But, as in Edith Martin's story from Carolina, the distinction between work and leisure is not so clearly defined. The back porch is about work, but the impression to be given off on the front porch is also about work.

Nevertheless, the work done on the front porch is much more "presentable" than the work accomplished on the back porch. It is, to use Edith Martin's words, "more fun than work." In keeping with community rules of decorum, fish are not gutted on cemetery slabs; instead, beans are snapped, quilt pieces are stitched, and ice cream—itself a nonessential pleasure food—is cranked. On this front porch, as the family intersects with the community, we see a much more integrated approach to leisure and work, while the back porch seems grounded largely in family chores. Indeed, "no lollygagging [is] allowed," and "loitering children [are] not encouraged or tolerated." As Gallagher has said, "Back porches were serious, open-air work parlors." Notice, though, that Gallagher uses the word "parlor," which is the "showroom" of a home's interior, designated for entertaining. Even while fish are gutted and family chores are done, we are aware that the back porch is, to some degree, about community display and socializing with others.

In the previous accounts, the boundaries between the "back region" and the "front region" are not nearly as tidy as Goffman theorized. This blurring of boundaries comes from the very liminality of both front and back porches, which are, to varying degrees, "betwixt and between" family and community. If the lines between public and private are blurred on the porch, lines between "public" social activities and "private" work activities will also shift.

What is most significant about the uses of these front and back porches is how their liminality facilitates the creation of a southern identity that is grounded in an ethos of community and family. The lines between work and play will be hard to draw because, when family and neighbors come together on porches, socializing necessarily comes along in the form of sharing tasks, of telling stories, of gossip, and of watching the goings-on of the world outside. And if the front and back porches of these two accounts are used differently, that proves how individuals possess a certain privilege to create a "space" for themselves on their porches. However, this privilege must be negotiated within the rules of decorum in the South, which means that the impression displayed on the front porch must be "nicer" than the impression communicated from the back porch, even if "niceness" comes in varying degrees and is inevitably tied to class status. Southern culture is about sustaining images—often romanticized images—of itself and its people, and front porches are often engaged to communicate an image of togetherness, hospitality, and community—often, but not always.

Eugene Walter, in his 1998 New Yorker essay, "Secrets of a Southern Porch," recalled his grandmother's highly individualistic way of presenting herself on her front porch in Mobile, Alabama:

> In my childhood, the porch was a concept as well as a place. In Mobile, Alabama, everybody would always sit on the front porch shelling peas and exchanging the neighborhood gossip. If my grandmother sat facing the street, that meant she would "receive": other ladies, across the street, next door, or passing by, could come up on the porch and talk to her.
>
> If she sat sidewise, with her profile to the street, you could greet her and speak to her from the sidewalk but you couldn't come up onto the porch. If she was with her back to the street, she was invisible. It meant that she was reading the paper or hadn't done her hair yet. You wouldn't say anything to her. (60)

This grandmother's porch traditions indeed remind us that community norms of hospitality must be negotiated with individual eccentricities.

Norms must also be negotiated with the larger political structure. The foregoing stories recall a period when segregation in the South was, if not legal, then de facto. They remind us of an era when a woman was typically confined to the home and often under her husband's control. Zora Neale Hurston's novel Their Eyes Were Watching God illustrates just how porches can be used as "places" (to invoke de Certeau again) to control others. But even while porches are "places" of power struggles, Hurston ends her novel by showing that a person can work to overcome this "place," making it an individual "space" to express an identity. In her novel, set in Eatonville, Florida, during the 1930s, Hurston brings together many of our concerns in this chapter—storytelling, community, family, and identity. And these concerns get played out on various front and back porches in the all-black, self-governing community of Eatonville—Hurston's hometown.

FRONT AND BACK PORCHES IN THE WORK OF ZORA NEALE HURSTON

Their Eyes Were Watching God tells the life story of Janie Crawford, a thirtyish African American woman in the 1930s who has just returned to her hometown

Living the Everyday Life

of Eatonville, Florida, after having left with a young man, Tea-Cake Woods, not long after her husband, Jody Starks, died. Hurston's narrative reveals the porch dynamics of a special geographical region by setting her story in one of the few all-black, self-governing towns in the Jim Crow South. This setting means that the social conflicts played out on the porch are more intraracial than interracial. Janie is struggling to define herself within the African American community that has, until now, rejected her because of her class status. Janie's first husband, Jody, had been mayor of the town, so Janie was expected to conform to her public role of "mayor's wife." Needless to say, running off with a younger man soon after her husband died violated Eatonville's notions of "proper behavior." Janie is definitely not giving off the right "impression," according to her neighbors.

On the day that Janie returns to Eatonville, the community has gathered on Pheoby Watson's porch to witness the event. Hurston doesn't separate the community from the site, saying that "the porch couldn't talk for looking" (2). It soon recovers from its acute aphasia; this is a southern porch whose common experiences and actions are of "puttin' they mouf on things they don't know nothin' about" (6), or, in other words, a porch that creates community cohesion largely through gossiping and telling stories. And no storytelling session is more mouth-watering than one having to do with the just-returned Janie in her "over-hauls," a woman who has dared, according to the convictions of the porch, to step outside "her own class" to marry the lower-class Tea-Cake Woods.

Janie returns to Eatonville, and it is on the steps of her own back porch where, "full of that oldest human longing—self revelation" (6), Janie tells her life story to her friend Pheoby. There are several significant porches in Hurston's novel. As we just saw, there is Pheoby's gossiping porch, which represents the folk community that has Janie "up in they mouth" to pelt her with unasked questions. There is the performing porch of Joe Starks's store, a male-dominated society where men pass "around the pictures of their thoughts for the others to look at and see" (48). There is Janie's own front porch where Jody, obsessed with "impression management," commands his wife to look like "a pretty doll-baby" (28). And this front porch stands in contrast to the intimacy of Janie's back porch, symbolic of the private world of Janie's intimate personal narrative to Pheoby. Each porch situates Janie differently in relation to her community.

Janie's position as story listener on the store porch says much about her eventual self-discovery. Janie is in conflict with a male-centered society whose members see themselves as the "privileged storytellers," able to deliver the "crayon enlargements of life." Moreover, Janie's husband, Joe Starks, owns and pretty well dominates this porch. He consciously excludes her from the ongoing male storytelling sessions by forcing her to go indoors. Consequently, she has come to "hate the inside of that store" largely because it symbolizes the dominance that has caused her loneliness (51). Janie hears "big long laughs from the porch" and finds herself "wallowing in it" (65). At this point in her life, she longs to be an integral part of the store porch, to find a "space" in this "place" owned by her husband, "the mayor." At one point, Janie throws herself into the conversation to philosophize about God's relationship to women and to alert the male community to how little they understand this relationship, despite their attempts to appear "all-knowing":

> Sometimes God gits familiar wid us womenfolks too and talks His inside business. He told me how surprised He was 'bout y'all turning out so smart after Him makin' yuh different, and how surprised y'all is goin' tuh be if you ever find out you don't know half as much 'bout us as you think you do. It's so easy to make yo'self out God Almighty when you ain't got nothin' tuh strain against but women and chickens. (70–71)

Janie fully understands how cultural norms, which shape this site as male, work against her. But Jody doesn't appreciate Janie's philosophizing in public, warning her that she is "gettin' too moufy" (71). On Jody's store porch, she is forced to listen because she is not only a woman, she is a woman who is a victim of Jody's own "impression management." He insists on classing her as "the mayor's wife."

The store porch in an African American community is, to use Robert Hemenway's words, "the totem representing black cultural tradition; it is where the values of the group are manifested in verbal behavior" (23). In her autobiography, *Dust Tracks on a Road*, Hurston, herself a folklorist, tells of the significance of Joe Clarke's (the prototype for Jody Starks) porch in her hometown of Eatonville:

> Men sat around the store on boxes and benches and passed this world and the next one through their mouths. The right and the wrong, the who, when and why was passed on, and nobody doubted the conclusions. . . . There were no discreet nuances of life on Joe Clarke's porch. There were open kindnesses, anger, hate, love, envy and its kinfolks, but all emotions were naked, and

nakedly arrived at. . . . For me, the store porch was the most interesting place that I could think of. I was not allowed to sit around there, naturally. But, I could and did drag my feet going in and out, whenever I was sent there for something, to allow whatever was being said to hang in my ear. (61–62)

Picturing the young Zora dragging her feet so that the life of the porch would hang in her ears helps us to envision Janie's own desire to be part of the store porch. But she cannot. One of her sustained desires is to create a "space" for herself in this male society. Indeed, Janie is outside the male and female communities of Eatonville.

Janie has grown up with no siblings, nor does she ever become a central part of Eatonville's female population. If this chapter has generalized about southerners' privileging family and community, Janie's life stands to remind us that there are always exceptions to valid generalizations. Janie is, for all intents and purposes, bereft of family, and she is not an integral part of Eatonville's community. With the exception of Pheoby, the women in this community typically perceive Janie as the "bell cow" different from the rest of the "gang" (39), a distinction that issues from her color as well as her gender. Janie's light skin and long hair have also led Joe Starks to class her off: If she is not inside the store, she is consigned to her own front porch by Jody and "made to . . . rock and fan [her]self and eat p'taters dat other folks plant just special for [her]" (28). Jody ensures that Janie will fan herself on an imposing front porch. The words of the Eatonville community reveal the dominance of the Starkses' home. They say:

Take for instance that new house of his. It had two stories with porches, with banisters and such things. The rest of the town looked like servants' quarters surrounding the "big house." And different from everybody else in the town he put off moving in until it had been painted, in and out. And look at the way he painted it—a gloaty, sparkly white. The kind of promenading white that the houses of Bishop Whipple, W. B. Jackson and the Vanderpools wore. It made the village feel funny talking to him—just like he was anybody else. (44)

The community claims that "it was bad enough for white people, but when one of your own color could be so different it put you on a wonder" (45). Unlike the porches that we read about earlier in this chapter, porches that to varying degrees link family members to others in the community, the Starkses' porch is just that—*stark*. This porch is not a link to the town; it is a barrier to protect and preserve Jody's class status. Though Janie should theoretically feel more connected to the community on this transitional site, she is instead set apart as a spectacle for public viewing. Because Jody is using Goffman's notion of "impression management" to overpower the individual desires of his wife, the house porch becomes a "place," a tyrannical "front region," that separates Janie from the rest of Eatonville. There is no leisurely waving and greeting and churning of ice cream on this front porch. Janie silently fights against exclusive social practices that endorse light skin, class dominance, and male privilege, but the community members endorse her consignment to the front porch. According to them, "she slept with authority and so she was part of it in [their] mind" (44).

When Jody dies, Janie inherits the porches that have been controlled by her husband. She doesn't wait terribly long to begin to shift the terms of the porches' power: Rather than allowing them to be "places" for others to control her, she reframes them as "spaces" for her own self-discovery. It is no wonder that one of Janie's first acts of self-liberation is to sit on *her* store porch during the evenings. She does not change the physical features of the space, "except of evenings she sat on the porch and listened" (85). Janie means to situate herself squarely within her community's cultural traditions and to reinvent the porch's typically male power in her own terms. She no doubt astounds the townspeople when she and Tea-Cake play a game of Florida flip on what was once Jody's store porch. Her notions of what impression she wants to give off are radically changing.

Engaged in active listening and no longer a mere "fixture," Janie begins to assert her individual power by inviting others onto the front porch of her house, as well as by limiting its availability to potential suitors. Indeed, "six months of wearing black passed and not one suitor had ever gained the house porch" (87). Perhaps her greatest act of subversion is to tell her personal narrative to Pheoby on her own back porch. Pheoby enters the private "space" of Janie's backyard, her home's "back region," through "the intimate gate" (4), which symbolizes her entry into the private, intimate "space" of Janie's unique personal narrative. Janie's storytelling world with Pheoby reminds us that back porches are different from front porches because they are not part of the public arena: They are personal realms for private concerns, whereas front porches are "breast pockets" for the public to view.

By retreating to Janie's back porch for Janie to tell her life story to her best friend, the two women are able temporarily to escape some of the public constraints of Janie's store porch and of her own front porch. They are able to suspend requirements of "impression management" to create a more intimate "space" for their storytelling event. Finally, Janie has gained a useful stage in Eatonville. On what is now her own real property, she is the authorized teller of her own story, largely because of the space she now owns and negotiates. And through her storytelling to another community member, she is able, on this back porch of her own, to forge an individual identity.

But lest we imagine that Janie is using her back porch to completely separate herself from her surrounding community, Hurston lets us know that Janie's life story will eventually get connected to the community at large. It will do so through Pheoby's appropriation and eventual retelling of Janie's story. Janie's back porch, while separated, thus serves as a transitional "space" between private and public worlds: Janie's story, through Pheoby's "hungry listening," will become part of the community mythology. Pheoby, eager to "feel and do through Janie," finds herself "dialat[ing] all over with eagerness" (7), and, after the telling, she has "growed ten feet higher from jus' listening" (182). Because she recounts her story for an effective listener and reliable reteller, Janie has managed to exert control over the tale for future retellings. She not only communicates the details of her story, but also proposes suitable ways for Pheoby to "retell" the story: She warns Pheoby, for example, that "you must tell 'em dat love ain't something lak uh grindstone dat's de same thing everywhere." Rather, "it takes its shape from de shore it meets, and it's different with every shore" (182). Janie knows that her story will become part of community gossip, and she tells the story with the full awareness of how it should be shaped to accommodate community norms.

Janie's ultimate presence as a community storyteller indicates her path to black womanhood, wherein she establishes what bell hooks calls, in *Talking Back*, a "liberational voice." As hooks asserts, "Moving from silence into speech is for the oppressed, the colonized, the exploited, and those who stand and struggle side by side a gesture of defiance that heals, that makes new life and growth possible. It is that act of speech of 'talking back,' that is no mere gesture of empty words, that is the expression of our movement from object to subject—the liberated voice" (9). Reshaping the front and back porches of her life, changing them from overpowering "places" to vital "spaces" for herself, Janie "talks back" to confront community constraints of class, gender, and race.

Hurston's novel begins to introduce us to the less romantic side of the porch, to social situations where porches can function as exclusionary "places." Thus, Hurston invites us to examine more thoroughly the ways in which porches not only bring families and communities closer together but act to separate them as well.

3: SETTING BOUNDARIES OF RACE & CLASS

have already said that this book works at the intersection of spatial and social practices, investigating how the porch is a liminal space between public and private, self and other, individual and community. Because in the South the racial is part and parcel of the spatial and the social, and because class is inevitably bound up with race, any look at how the porch regulates social boundaries should account for the intricate interweaving of race, class, and culture in the South. (Of course, as Hurston's novel *Their Eyes Were Watching God* has already indicated, questions of race and class are inevitably entangled in gender matters, and the discussion here will surely raise questions of gender. But I will give more particular attention to the relationship between the porch and gender roles in Chapter 4.)

To advance a discussion of how the porch applies pressure to matters of race and class, the most useful place to begin is with the architectural history of the porch, which, as I briefly mentioned in the first chapter, is as racially complicated as the South. Indeed, it is because the porch's history is inextricably tied to race that I have delayed the historical discussion until now.

PORCH HISTORY

Architectural histories of the domestic porch are few and far between and are usually speculative. This scarcity of thorough research on the house porch is grounded partly in the architectural historian's routine privileging of elite buildings and structures. As historian of vernacular architecture John Michael Vlach has said, "Too often our view of architecture is focused solely on the unique monumental structures designed in large part to display the wealth and power of the elite." He points to researchers who have given attention to "grand mansions, churches, and government buildings together with other public structures" and claims that "the greatest portion of the built environment—the houses that most people live in—goes unnoticed." Because African influences are seen most strongly in vernacular art and architecture in the United States, such exclusions of everyday buildings and structures have historically overlooked the rich legacy of African influences in American architecture. Vlach insists that "when studies of architecture are expanded to embrace the totality of the built environment—all buildings great and small—the impact of an Afro-American tradition in architecture becomes evident" (*Afro-American Tradition* 122). And, of course, our particular concern here is with the impact of African American traditions on the southern domestic porch.

To account for the porch's racial history, I have relied heavily on research conducted by John Michael Vlach and by Jay Edwards. Both of these researchers have maintained that the southern porch has origins in African architecture. For example, in establishing the full-front gallery as an African architectural form, Edwards says the following:

> Before the coming of the Europeans, the indigenous domestic architectures of the tropical Coasts of the Gulf of Guinea, between Cape Mersurado and Old Calibar and as far south as Angola, were characterized by rectangular buildings. Some were constructed low to the ground, but many were raised on platforms or pillars, with open walls or gallery-like structures incorporated into them. (23)

Thus Edwards claims that West African housing had porchlike structures even before Europeans began to colonize the continent. How the southern porch in the United States was influenced by African-style architecture is, as Vlach says, "not simple and direct" (*Work* 186). Vlach, however, has offered convincing evidence to show that free blacks from Haiti, who themselves were former African slaves, figured centrally in the importation of African architecture to the southern United States, particularly in the development of the shotgun house in New Orleans, with its commanding front porch (*Work* 186).

In essence, the shotgun house, which was first defined by Fred B. Kniffen in 1936 as "one room in width and from one to three or more rooms deep, with frontward-facing gable" (186), developed in New Orleans in the late eighteenth century with the massive immigration of free blacks from Haiti. After the slave revolt in Haiti, led by Toussaint L'Ouverture in 1791, free Haitians began to stream into the United States. By 1810, New Orleans had over 3,000 free people of color, over 4,000 slaves, and only 12,000 people overall. As Vlach said, "The influx of

Houses at Cape Mersurado, Grain Coast, West Africa, ca. 1700: (a) hut; (b) kitchen;
(c) granary for millet and rice; (d) palaver (men's talking) room; (e) courtyard.
(Drafted by Mary Lee Eggert, 1999; courtesy of the Fred B. Kniffen
Cultural Resources Lab, Louisiana State University, Baton Rouge)

Haitian immigrants made New Orleans a truly black city," one in which free
blacks early realized a degree of economic success (*Work* 194).

Most significant here is that the former Haitian slaves brought with them the
architecture of slave cabins, namely the shotgun house, or *ti-kay* (*petite caille*),
with its front porch. And where Haitian slave housing is involved, African architecture is necessarily implicated. Haitian slaves depended particularly on the
two-room houses of the Yoruba in West Africa. Saying that the porch was added
to the shotgun house in Haiti does not imply that porches were absent in West
African architecture. I have already quoted evidence from Jay Edwards suggesting that they were present. And Afolabi Ojo offers similar evidence in his article
"Traditional Yoruba Architecture." He says:

Overlooking the [Yoruba] courtyard is the veranda or piazza which runs
throughout the building on the inner side of the compound. The veranda can
be as wide as eight feet. It is an intensively used part of the house. It is used
in the same way as the living room of modern houses in that all visitors are
received there. Mats, stools made of palm branches, and skins of animals are
hung on the walls along the veranda from which they are brought down and
set on the floor to seat important guests. In addition, all craft industries that

Decorated *ti kay* (shotgun house) in Port-au-Prince, Haiti.
(Photograph by Jay Edwards, 1995; courtesy of Jay Edwards)

Double shotgun house in New Orleans. (Photograph by Walker Evans, 1936; Library of Congress, Prints and Photographs Division [LC-USF342-TOI-008060-E])

are not totally carried on in open spaces away from the home take place along the veranda. Such important industries include hair-dressing, ginning, carving, and vertical-loom weaving by women and basket weaving, leather working and wood or calabash carving by men. . . . Human beings also share the veranda during the dry season when rooms may become unbearably hot. (15)

The African history of the shotgun house is further complicated by its resemblance to the housing of the Arawak Indians in the Dominican Republic. Called

Arawak *bohio*, Dominican Republic, sixteenth century. (After Gonzalo Fernández de Oviedo y Valdéz, *Historia General y Natural de las Indias, y las Tierra-Firma de Mar Océane* [1535; rpt., Madrid: Imprenta de la Real Academia de la Historia, 1851]; courtesy of the Fred B. Kniffen Cultural Resources Lab, Louisiana State University, Baton Rouge)

a *bohio* by the Spanish, the Arawak housing structure was similar to the shotgun structure. And the *bohio* even had a small porch (Vlach, *Work* 201), unlike the two-room Yoruba house. Vlach speculates that African slaves could have drawn on their own Yoruba-style housing and added elements of the Arawak *bohio*.

Although African influences on the front porch are evident, there are nevertheless European influences as well. We need only think of the imposing portico that graces Thomas Jefferson's Monticello to remember the influences of classical architecture on southern plantation homes. Jefferson relied on the architecture of Rome mainly because he wanted to reject the influence of England on American architecture. In incorporating the classical portico at Monticello, Jefferson, like other plantation owners, designed his house to be associated with the elite. In fact, even today the portico characterizes homes that offer the least inviting "porches."

Setting Boundaries

Monticello, the east portico. (Illustrated in *Century* magazine, May 1887;
Library of Congress, Prints and Photographs Division [LC-USZ62-104751])

Of course, there are exceptions. Henry Dauterive of New Iberia, Louisiana, is
pictured on the stately porch of his aunts, Elise and Mildred Weeks, of the famous Weeks family in New Iberia. The house is situated next to The Shadows on
the Teche, a Classical Revival plantation built by the Weeks family between 1831
and 1834 and now a vital stop on the tourism circuit of New Iberia. At the time
of our interview, in the summer of 1999, Dauterive told me that his aunts, before
they succumbed to illness, made frequent use of their stately portico, even visiting with neighbors. Having been lifelong residents of New Iberia, they were very
much an institution in the small town. But their portico is an exception, indeed.
Typically, a portico is an imposing structure that communicates, at the very least,
detachment from the community at large.

While the imposing portico originated in Europe, the broad, open front porch
of the everyday American home has no European counterparts. British homes,
for example, have only antechambers, bearing none of the social implications of
a full-front porch in the South. The houses of Charleston, South Carolina, which

Home of Elise and Mildred Weeks, New Iberia, La. Their nephew, Henry Dauterive, is pictured with the author. (Photograph by Jon Griffin Donlon, 1999)

are steeped in English architecture, demonstrate, according to Vlach, that for a long time after the British settled there, "extensive porches were outside of the Anglo-American repertoire of architectural forms" (*Afro-American Tradition* 137). Charleston homes do have characteristic side galleries. However, these side galleries did not become popular in Charleston until after 1790, when refugees from Haiti arrived. So even the side galleries of Charleston could have West Indian influences.

While stately porticoes in the eighteenth century characterized upper-class architecture in the South, the everyday full-front porch did not become common in the South until the slave population increased in the nineteenth century. Thus, Vlach speculates that the slaves themselves may have contributed to the development of the functional full-front porch as an escape from the heat. He says, "The front porch may be another manifestation of the common wisdom of black folk. Slaves might have added porches to their cabins as a matter of traditional architectural practice" (*Afro-American Tradition* 138).

Phillippe Oszuscik, in his article "Passage of the Gallery and Other Caribbean Elements from the French and Spanish to the British in the United States," offers a competing explanation of how the gallery made its way from the Gulf Coast, with its strong Caribbean connections, to the southeastern coast of the United States, with its strong English associations. Oszuscik claims that the first recorded American gallery dates back to 1702 in Old Mobile and that the form later made its way to the East Coast. Oszuscik argues that the movement from the Gulf to the East Coast could have followed several currents: British trade routes to the Caribbean; contact between the British and the Spanish in St. Augustine, dating back to 1568; the influence of the French Huguenots in South Carolina; the contact of British trappers with the French; the British inheritance of the Florida parishes in 1763; and the remainder of British citizens in Florida after the territory was ceded to Spain in 1781. Oszuscik claims that a strong possibility rests with the fact that France, Spain, and England came into contact with each other in the seventeenth and eighteenth centuries on small islands off Haiti and on Haiti itself in "buccaneer" communities. These communities comprised Europeans with Caribbean colonies and descendants of Arawaks, Caribs, and Africans (2). The British ultimately cultivated in eighteenth-century America what Oszuscik calls a "French-British Creole" gallery style that has not been recog-

Gallery and garden, Charleston, S.C., ca. 1920. (Detroit Publishing Company,
no. 0272471; Gift, State Historical Society of Colorado, 1949; Library of Congress,
Prints and Photographs Division [LC-D4-72471])

nized by scholars because, first, many records are housed in London and, second, no actual cottages survive today. This style consisted of exterior stairs and
complete two-story verandas (6).

Admittedly, much of this architectural history is speculative, as I have already
mentioned. Nevertheless, we can say with full assurance that, whatever the currents that generated the construction of the front porch on the Gulf and East

Setting Boundaries

Coasts, Afro-Caribbean influences weighed heavily on the development of this important domestic structure. We can also say that the porch, in its broadest sense—including the full-front porch, the partial-front porch, the side gallery, and the classical portico—bears the stamp of Africa, of Europe, of the Caribbean, and possibly of Arawak Indians in Haiti.

Thus, the southern porch is, to whatever degree and from whatever origin, a hybrid, "creolized" structure in that different cultural influences have, throughout history, come together to influence its development. If ever southern culture has provided us with a vernacular structure to manifest the complexities of racial interaction in the South, the porch is the genuine article: Its very history bespeaks cultural miscegenation. And if the history of the porch itself is entangled in hybridity, then the culture of the people who occupy those porches must likewise be a matter of creolization.

"CREOLIZED" CULTURE

The complicated "creolization" of the porch, itself, certainly reflects the hybrid that is southern culture. The paradoxical "shared-yet-separate" nature of racial interaction in the American South has historically bound southern communities together, resulting in degrees of cultural miscegenation, while nevertheless setting physical and psychological limits to the cultivation of interracial intimacy, resulting in separate racial communities. Unlike many northerners, most southerners, both black and white, are, even if unconsciously, engaged with the other race, in spite of legacies of racial segregation. The appropriation of European culture by African Americans, together with the infusion of African culture into white southern culture, has constructed a tapestry of multiracial threads inextricably interwoven.

W. J. Cash has discussed such intermingling of cultures in his classic *The Mind of the South*, in which he describes the relationships of nineteenth-century blacks and whites as "nothing less than organic." Slaves were compelled to reframe their very existences in terms of the "New World," while "nearly the whole body of whites, young and old, had constantly before their eyes the example, had constantly in their ears the accent, of the Negro." He claims that "Negro entered into white man as profoundly as white man entered into Negro—subtly influencing every gesture, every word, every emotion and idea, every attitude" (51). Ralph Ellison, in his essay "The World and the Jug," echoes Cash's assertion, saying that "Southern whites cannot walk, talk, sing, conceive of laws or justice, think of sex, love, the family or freedom without responding to the presence of Negroes" (*Shadow* 116).

There is a large body of literature devoted to tracing the degrees and directions of influences and entanglements in Anglo and African cultures in America. Melville Herskovits's famous publication in 1941, *The Myth of the Negro Past*, pioneered such studies by tracing the retention of Africanisms in black American culture. Although his study was limited by his focus on the Caribbean and on South America for evidence, he did establish fundamental syncretist theories of African retentions and reinterpretations in the New World, and he did help to debunk the myth that African Americans were devoid of a cultural past. Herskovits looked at both secular and religious life for specific examples of African retentions, from walking styles to ways of farming, hairdressing, display in religious services, folktales, dialect, and—important to our focus here—to Voodoo.

In 1958 Richard Dorson published *American Negro Folktales* and challenged the claim that black folklore was of Africanist origin, asserting that the stories he collected had European roots. In 1963 E. Franklin Frazier further disputed Herskovits's study with his book *The Negro Church in America*. Frazier, like Dorson, was suspicious of claiming pure Africanist origins of black folklore and culture, and he maintained that slavery destroyed African customs. His position was that, because of the close interaction with whites, the slaves were forced to displace African culture and substitute social patterns adopted for survival in America.

Though no one would deny that Africans on this continent have been compelled to appropriate European cultural traditions, Frazier's and Dorson's negations of African cultural influences in America are generally no longer accepted as authoritative. Many anthropologists have worked to extend Herskovits's ethnography by looking at how Africanisms have helped to construct black and white American cultures. One of the most recent is a collection of essays edited by Joseph Holloway and titled *Africanisms in American Culture* (1990). Indeed, John Edward Philips's essay "The African Heritage of White America" provocatively suggests that "as much African culture survives now among whites as among blacks in the United States . . . especially in the South" (225). He examines uses of the banjo, yodeling, non-Christian belief systems, borrowed traditions of generosity and elaborate etiquette, and slang as examples of African aspects of white culture. And, in so doing, Philips attempts to reconcile the Herskovits-Frazier debate by saying that Herskovits was correct in arguing for the survival of African culture, but Frazier was also correct in claiming that Africanisms are not "the distinguishing characteristic of African-American society" (227).

Holloway's collection comes out of such seminal studies as Lorenzo Turner's *Africanisms in the Gullah Dialect* (1949), which broke important ground by being the first to examine linguistic retentions of Africanisms among black southerners who live on the Sea Islands off the South Carolina coast, and J. L. Dillard's *Black English* (1972), which claims that "it was the [white] Southerner, and almost exclusively the [white] Southern child, who really learned the Negro's variety of English" (198). Dillard is careful to remind us, though, that many southern blacks have, since the days of slavery, negotiated between dialect and "Standard" English, pointing out that "a Negro of the nineteenth century spoke or did not speak the non-standard dialect—or Plantation Creole—according to his social position and background." And as William Labov finally puts it, "Almost every feature of Black English Vernacular can be found among some white speakers in the South" (*Language* 8).

The South, then, has created a fabric that interweaves black and white cultures in a multitude of ways. Of course, these threads will vary from culture to culture, class to class, gender to gender, and region to region. The following stories, set in "the truly black city" of New Orleans, show how the porch can reflect that city's distinctive creolized heritage.

"KEEP THE FRONT DOOR OPEN BUT THE SCREEN DOOR LOCKED"

Kenyada Corley, an African American woman in her early twenties who was mentioned in Chapter 1, talked at length during our interview about how her paternal grandmother, Rosie Lee Corley, used her New Orleans shotgun home —indeed her front porch—to reflect the Afro-Caribbean influence on African American culture in New Orleans, particularly in Mrs. Corley's Voodoo practices. Mrs. Corley, who lived on Garrard Street, was the mother of Kenyada's biological father, who now lives in Trinidad. Kenyada, a former Zulu Queen of the New Orleans Mardi Gras, has always called her stepfather "dad," but she remained close to her grandmother.

Voodoo, or, as it is called in Haitian Creole, *Vodou*, remains a legitimate religion, practiced by the majority of the contemporary Haitian population. The word *Voodoo* can be traced to *Vodu* in the language of the Fon peoples of West

Africa, specifically in the country of Benin, formerly known as Dahomey. Three West African tribes—the Yoruba of Nigeria, the Fon of the present-day Benin (Dahomey), and the Kongo of the present-day Democratic Republic of Congo (Zaire) and Angola—seem to have most strongly influenced Haitian Voodoo, which eventually made its way to the United States with the immigration of free blacks and the importation of Haitian slaves. New Orleans, in particular, felt the effects of Haitian Voodoo practices, still a vital presence today. I do not want to suggest that Voodoo survives only in New Orleans. Gloria Naylor's exceptional novel *Mama Day*, which we will examine more closely, represents how Voodoo is practiced on the Sea Islands off the coast of South Carolina and Georgia. Moreover, Voodoo made its way to New York, Miami, and even to Montreal. Nevertheless, New Orleans, complete with tours of Marie Laveau's house and gift shops in the French Quarter, is still a center for the Afro-Caribbean practices.

Because of the influence of French Catholicism, Voodoo in the West Indies and in New Orleans has been syncretized with Christianity. Mrs. Corley, before her recent death, belonged to the Baptist church in New Orleans; nonetheless, she exercised religious practices held over from Voodoo, practices taught to her by her parents from Trinidad. As Kenyada said, "[My grandmother] never really went to church. She formulated her own type of religion." Kenyada listened to stories, for example, of how Mrs. Corley got her husband by putting a hex on him. But while she practiced Voodoo to her advantage, most of her practices arose out of anxiety and dread, to protect herself from evil. For example, on every Friday the 13th, Mrs. Corley, according to Kenyada, put broomstraw in her hair and took to her bed to protect herself from evil. Or she would refuse to move furniture in August, doing so only in September. Her fear of danger might have been because her own mother "was poisoned by a lady who was in love with the husband," and her father was murdered as well.

Kenyada often went to local shops with her grandmother in order to purchase materials for Voodoo practices. And Kenyada remembers her grandmother using these materials on her front porch in New Orleans, a "really long, concrete porch on a shotgun house—camelback." While her grandmother "burned a lot of candles in the house," she burned incense on her porch. When I asked Kenyada if doing so was part of her religious practices, she said: "She had 'power' that she burned in a glass dish. And if it went out, she had a fit because she hated to relight it. If it went out on its own, that was fine, but if you blew it out, she would have a fit. She had 'green power' in a long ashtray. You could open it up so the ashes would fall inside." Giving her front porch an ethnic identity, expressive of African, Caribbean, and American influences, Mrs. Corley used her "creolized" porch to protect herself and her home from the evils that could cross the threshold. But despite its distinctive ethnic characteristics, her porch was defined by everyday, mundane activities. Kenyada remembers "playing jacks" with her sister on their grandmother's front porch and listening to their grandmother's daily aphorisms, such as "life is hard" and "Mama may have and Papa may have but God bless the child who has his own."

Kenyada, calling her grandmother a neighborhood matriarch, recounted the following porch story: "A young guy went up to my grandmother and asked for a cigarette. My grandmother was like, 'You can take these cigarettes, but make sure you work and you get a job and you pay me.' And my sister told me that, like, five years later that guy came back and gave my grandmother a cigarette plus $10.00." Mrs. Corley was part of the black middle class in New Orleans, and, as such, she used her porch as a conduit to the community. In addition, she wanted to influence others—particularly young people—for the better. She must have carried some authority in her advice to the young man in order for him to have remembered her five years later.

Mrs. Corley also heard much of the community gossip while rocking on her front porch. As Kenyada said:

Every time something went on, someone in the neighborhood came to her to tell her. I always wondered, "How did she always know what was going on in the neighborhood. She never went anywhere!" But people would come and tell her. She would always say, "When you open your door, trash will come in. The key to that is to keep the front door open, but the screen door locked. That way they have to ring the bell."

One wonders whom, in her general use of "trash," Mrs. Corley was excluding from her home's interior. Young men looking for money? Gossipmongers? Poor whites? Was she even including the white insurance salesmen who often came to knock on her door? After all, they were rarely able to cross Mrs. Corley's threshold. Kenyada said:

Most of [my grandmother's] insurance agents were white. They would never come inside. Just lately, I mean the last two years, she would let them come into the living room, but they could never go any further than that. And we found out that her insurance policy wasn't that good. I mean it paid only $800 or so. She had so many insurance policies—burial, life—but they weren't worth anything.

In my interviews with African Americans, I have not come across stories of whites socializing on the porches of blacks. And I have not talked to any white people who felt comfortable going into black neighborhoods to drink iced tea or sip lemonade on front porches. But I have heard several accounts of how white people, particularly white men, came onto black porches to conduct business, primarily to sell insurance or to sell lottery tickets. For example, Penny Breazeale, a New Orleans Creole, tells the following story, set in the Seventh Ward of New Orleans in the 1960s:

There was a white guy who would come around every Tuesday, in the evening, and he would go from porch to porch. The Seventh Ward is a community, at the time that I grew up, where all the craftsmen and laborers—people who were tilesetters, who were carpenters, who were plumbers, all the crafts of building—this is where they lived. And they passed on their traditions from one family to the next. So when you went into the houses in the Seventh Ward, you'd be very surprised at how elaborately built they were, how much tilework they had in them, because that's the kind of work that they did.

But I can remember that on Tuesdays, you'd see this little guy named Raymond, and I was a little child, seeing him go from door to door. And I never could understand what he was doing. He was never allowed inside the door, but he would stay on the porch. And it wasn't until I was a teenager that it became illegal to have the lottery man come to your door. That's who Raymond was. He "visited" on everybody's porch. The only white people that would come in the neighborhood were the lottery man and the insurance man. They wanted to pretend like he was somebody else. We didn't know who he was. We knew he wasn't the insurance man because the insurance man always came with his book. Insurance men sold mostly burial policies. How you were put away at death was very important—and still is—in the black community.

Though the young-looking Raymond turned out to be the "lottery man," the young Penny had to first rule out the "insurance man" because his history is a long one in the black community.

Allan Gurganus's novella Blessed Assurance reveals this history of exploitation throughout the South. The story recounts the days of "Jerry," who, as a nineteen-year-old, collected "assurance" payments in a Carolina milltown. As he mounts the steps of porches in "Baby Africa" to do his exploitative business, Jerry's task is to collect fifty cents a week from policyholders. As Jerry says: "My territory was a town of shacks. With dogs at every one. . . . I sprinted from my black Nash up onto a rickety front porch. I knocked, panting, whipping out the book. One very old woman seemed to peek from every door" (237). If the policyholder skipped two payments, however, all policies, paid or unpaid, were forfeited. Jerry, the son of millworkers, eventually becomes an economic success, but the nightmares of having reported delinquent policyholders continue to haunt him fifty years later.

Given Gurganus's disturbing portrait of "assurance" collectors, one indeed wonders just what Mrs. Corley meant by "trash." Whatever her meaning, though, she meant to police the boundaries of her front porch, even protecting it with some added "green power," which burned steadily.

There is little doubt that in her use of "trash," Mrs. Corley included both blacks and whites. The authority with which she put in his place the young black man who borrowed cigarettes demonstrates that she felt some distinctions within her own racial community. New Orleans, in fact, is well known for its class and color distinctions within the African American community. The light-skinned Creole population, which descended largely from free blacks, distinguishes itself, even today, from darker-skinned African Americans. Penny Breazeale, who gave us the story about the "lottery man," is a light-skinned Creole from the Seventh Ward of New Orleans. We heard in her story about the impressive skills of the residents who lived in the Seventh Ward when she was growing up. In the following description of her neighborhood, she makes existing color divisions in New Orleans even clearer:

The Seventh Ward is a community of people that has a tremendous amount of French influence. Most of the people who lived in the Seventh Ward when I was growing up were from the river parishes, St. James and St. John Parishes, and because you had the riverboat that came in—just like a port, the Port of New Orleans—in that port you had most of your French ships that were coming in along the river. So the African women took up with men from the boat. The way I look [light-skinned] is from being part of that community. A lot of the way we did things in the Seventh Ward was how they would've been influenced by the French.

There is a strong likelihood that free blacks from Haiti also came into this port, further creolizing the culture. The long history of light-skinned free blacks in New Orleans has created a protracted history of intraracial segregation. Some people even now talk of the "paper bag" test, meaning that those with skin darker than a paper bag were excluded from certain social opportunities controlled by lighter-skinned African Americans.

But, of course, this intraracial tension isn't limited to New Orleans, to Louisiana, or even to America. (When my husband and I lived in Africa, for example, our flatmate, a brown-skinned woman from Botswana, routinely talked about her skin being "too dark" for her taste.) These long-standing barriers grounded in skin color among African Americans, which are inevitably tied to notions of class, get played out effectively in Ernest Gaines's novel *Catherine Carmier*. And Gaines uses front porches to symbolize the intraracial class conflicts in his fictional community of Bayonne, Louisiana.

"ON THE PORCH ALONE"

Alice Walker said in one of her essays, "It is a credit to a writer like Ernest J. Gaines, a black writer who writes mainly about the people he grew up with in rural Louisiana, that he can write about whites and blacks exactly as he sees them and knows them, instead of writing of one group as a vast malignant lump and the other as a conglomerate of perfect virtues" (*In Search* 19). Ernest Gaines, in all of his novels, depicts intraracial divisions, but he does so particularly well in *Catherine Carmier*. In his candid representation of intracommunity struggles, Gaines reminds us, through his symbolic uses of the front porch, that the black community is not monolithic but one with its own class boundaries, producing "many [black] Souths."

Robert Carmier, the Creole grandfather of Catherine Carmier, made history in the town of Bayonne by riding up to the local plantation store and asking Mack

Grover—who was "considered the best of the Grovers by the Negroes, the worst Grover by the whites" (9)—for permission to rent the house that had once belonged to the plantation's white overseer. No other white man wanted to live in the house, and the Grovers, who owned the plantation, had refused to rent it to blacks, so it had remained stubbornly vacant. Robert Carmier wanted this "big house," in particular, because he knew that he could farm "as well as any man and better than most" (8). Mack Grover reluctantly consented, believing that Robert Carmier could not succeed, "no matter how white he [was]" (11).

Robert Carmier and his family did succeed in farming. But they failed miserably at being part of the black community that populated the sharecroppers' quarters—a community of which Gaines himself had been a part and which he had valued. The southern ethos that authorizes community, characteristic of both black and white southern populations, certainly did not apply to the Carmier family. Their daily routine was as follows:

> Morning until night, six days a week, they were in the field. Then every Sunday morning, they got into the buggy and went to the Catholic church in Bayonne. Around five in the afternoon they would return, change into everyday clothes, and sit out on the porch. They visited no one, and no one in the quarters would dare visit them. Every so often one of the daughters would come in from Bayonne or New Orleans, but the rest of the time, Robert and his family, the four of them, would be seen on the porch alone. (12–13)

After Robert Carmier fights with one of the Cajun sharecroppers, he mysteriously disappears and is never seen again. His son Raoul, Catherine's oppressive father, takes over the farming and marries Della Johnson, of whom his Creole family disapproves. Della, after all, "would stand on the porch or out in the garden, talking to you so long that you would have to say, 'Della, I just have to be getting home'" (14). Della tries to turn the Carmier's front porch into a social place tied to the community, but Raoul eventually beats her down until she sits "on the porch alone" just like the rest of the Carmiers.

The family resembles more of a lifeless spectacle than they do living, breathing human beings. They are obviously engaged in "impression management," to recall Goffman's discussion, but the question is, for whom? The family seems unconcerned with the opinions of their neighbors. From the outside the house is "big, old, paintless" and sits up on "wooden blocks at least three feet high.

Eight or nine wooden steps led up to a long and warped front porch" (42). A warped porch is by no means a showplace intended to impress others. Gaines seems to use the decrepit conditions of the Carmier house to symbolize Raoul's crippled sense of self—he knows he cannot gain the approval of local whites, and he stubbornly refuses to be black. Such an isolated position can only lead to a warped identity.

On one particular afternoon, the narrator describes the Carmier family in the following inanimate terms: "Catherine sat near the end of the porch; Della was next to her, near the door; and Raoul sat across from both of them. They had been sitting on the porch half an hour and there had not been a dozen words spoken between them. Every now and then Della would slap a mosquito with the piece of cloth that she had brought out of the house, but other than this, there was nothing from any one" (136). Gaines's portrayal here of such a desolate, isolated porch reveals the extent to which the Carmiers were "betwixt and between" black and white, unable to pave a path into either community in Bayonne. Liminality here is not a passage. It is a frozen position where the Carmiers can be seen, but they can never interact, not even with each other.

Their dreary, isolated porch stands in stark contrast to the vital, living porches of the sharecroppers' quarters. The porch of Charlotte Moses is particularly animated. Charlotte is the aunt of the central character, Jackson, who has just returned to Bayonne after completing his education in California. Jackson is, himself, in the liminal position of neither wanting to return to Bayonne nor leave it for any place else. But he is certain of his long-standing love for Catherine Carmier. Raoul, however, has long opposed the relationship because of Jackson's dark complexion.

As the novel opens, Jackson has just returned to Bayonne, and his Aunt Charlotte is beside herself with joy. Of course, she must plan a "welcome home" party for him. On the night of the party, the porch is a central place of socializing: "The people started coming up to the house around sundown, and by eight o'clock the house, the porch, and the yard were filled. Brother [Jackson's friend], who was in charge of seeing that everything went all right, was all over the place. First, you saw him in the kitchen, then the living room, then out on the porch, and finally in the yard. Then back on the porch, the living room, and the kitchen again" (59). This lively porch, abuzz with activity, contrasts sharply with the static, stagnant porch of the Carmiers' decrepit house. Both porches are about negotiating boundaries, but Charlotte Moses's porch is about welcoming her community to traverse those boundaries, as they go from house to yard and then back again. Raoul Carmier's porch is about rendering boundaries impermeable.

It is no wonder that, at the novel's conclusion, when the dark-skinned Jackson faces down Raoul to claim "possession" of the light-skinned Catherine, he confronts the oppressive Creole patriarch, Raoul, on the Carmier's front porch. As they physically struggle, one of Raoul's fists catches "Jackson on the shoulder, and Jackson fell back against the porch." Later, "Raoul slammed against the end of the porch, was stunned for a moment, and turned on Jackson again" (238). Jackson and Raoul, literally fighting it out on this liminal place, struggle to define the direction of movement from the porch: Will the family retreat indoors, taking Catherine prisoner inside to abide by the family tradition of prejudice? Or will she cross the threshold of this warped household, leaving the sheltered, intolerant "place" of Raoul Carmier?

Neither Jackson nor Raoul wins the struggle. Raoul falls in front of Catherine, but she refuses to leave with Jackson and returns inside. Gaines implies that because of Raoul's lost power, Catherine will eventually leave to join Jackson, but we are never really sure. We do know, however, that Raoul's power has been undermined and that the "place" of the Carmier porch is in transition of some sort. The optimistic reading is that when Catherine ultimately returns to Jackson, she will have rendered the place a useful "space" for herself. The porch, then, will lose its exclusionary status to become inclusive.

Raoul Carmier's porch has been exclusionary because of the history of cultural and biological miscegenation in the South. Light-skinned blacks, knowing full well that society gives preference to white skin, are sometimes led to use to their advantage what little power their skin color can grant them. They are inevitably tied to both the black and the white communities, sharing racial and cultural characteristics of both, but are inevitably discriminated against by both. Thus we are back to the "shared-yet-separate" nature of race relations in the South. And, in Ernest Gaines's work, we see how the porch so perfectly symbolizes the power struggles that result from such paradoxes of race.

Gaines's novel and the previous examples from the "truly black city" of New Orleans give voice to a deeply interwoven interracial population. But what about more segregated regions of the South? Gloria Naylor's novel Mama Day provides one glimpse into a racially separate, but still creolized, culture.

Naylor's novel is set in Willow Springs, a fictional sea island off the coast of South Carolina and Georgia. To construct this setting, Naylor has drawn from her research on the Gullah people who occupy this coastal region. The Gullah people are unique in that their customs, language, and architecture are palpably African. I referred earlier to the crucial work done by linguist Lorenzo Turner, whose ethnographic research documented African retentions in the Gullah language. Today, many of the actual Sea Islands have suffered from land development, but Naylor's novel creates an island that is still black-owned and black-populated. European culture has certainly affected the island. The patriarch of the island, Bascombe Wade, was a Norwegian slave owner who bought the slave Sapphira, a legendary conjure woman from West Africa whose magical powers, associated with the Voodoo that she would have brought with her on the slave ship, have been passed down through the generations. These powers ultimately pass to Sapphira's descendant, Miranda Day, otherwise known as "Mama Day," the spiritual healer for the modern-day people of Willow Springs. "Somehow, someway," Sapphira Wade "took" her freedom in the year 1823. The legends vary on the island as to how she got control. But "mixing it all together and keeping everything that done shifted down through the holes of time," the story has several stable elements: Bascombe Wade died; the residents own the deeds to the land; and Sapphira gave birth to seven sons, the seventh of whom also gave birth to seven sons (3). Mama Day, being the daughter of the seventh son of a seventh son, has through her magic healed the people of Willow Springs throughout her many decades on the earth.

Before he was either killed or deserted by Sapphira Wade (and, again, local legends offer many different versions), Bascombe Wade built a grand home on Willow Springs, which eventually transferred to the seven sons of Sapphira Wade, then to their seven sons, and ultimately to Mama Day and her sister Abigail. The house, called the "Other Place" by the locals, is treated with deep respect in the community because it has seen much sadness, much power, and indeed much magic. The porch of the Other Place allows those who enter to cross the threshold from the ordinary to the extraordinary.

No scene is more telling of the porch's extraordinary passage than when Mama Day takes Bernice, a local woman desperate to have a child, to the Other Place for a fertility rite. Mama Day has helped Bernice to prepare her body for the extraordinary ritual through natural herbal remedies which will make her body ready for childbearing. But there is no way to prepare Bernice's mind for the evening when Mama Day waits for her on the porch of the Other Place. During the ritual, Mama Day takes a freshly laid hen's egg and gives it to Bernice, who "takes the egg while the shell's still pulsing and wet, breaks it, and eats," only moments after it has exited the hen's opening. Then "with a nod," the two go inside, crossing the threshold into the world of African magic grounded in Voodoo. With "pine chips smoking on the fire blazing in the parlor hearth," making the air "steamy and sweet," and with "every shadow in the unlit room . . . dancing along the floor and walls," Mama Day places the naked Bernice on a table, rubs her body vigorously, making it receptive to life-giving forces, and then lines up the hen's opening with Bernice's vaginal opening, so that the egg the hen is laying can transfer directly into Bernice's body: "The uncountable, the unthinkable, is one opening. Pulsing and alive—wet—the egg moves from one space to the other. A rhythm older than woman draws it in and holds it tight" (139–40).

Strange cultural territory, indeed, if viewed from our ordinary, everyday positions. But when Mama Day takes Bernice across the threshold, she also allows the reader to cross the threshold into a distinct cultural territory that is more magical than real, more African than American, more symbolic than literal. By using the home of the slave-owning ancestor to practice her ancient, secret rituals, Mama Day transforms the "place" into her own creolized "space," where the powers of her African ancestors can give life. And it is important that this event is happening in Gullah territory, off the coast of South Carolina and Georgia, where African influences are still so deeply felt. The legacy of slavery and of European influences is integral to the history, so that even Mama Day's porch is a "shared-yet-separate" racial setting, invoking the legend not only of Sapphira Wade, but also of her one-time owner, Bascombe Wade. Nevertheless, the culture is deeply African, so that the biological and cultural infusions that Bascombe Wade might have contributed are secondary to Mama Day's gift to help Bernice.

ABIDING PARADOXES

This abiding paradox of "shared-yet-separate" racial relations exists, in part, because the concept of "culture" itself includes contradictory ideas of "constraint" and "mobility." As Stephen Greenblatt has theorized, "The ensemble of beliefs and practices that form a given culture function as a pervasive technology of control, a set of limits within which social behavior must be contained, a repertoire of models to which individuals must conform." Greenblatt further argues that "the limits need not be narrow . . . but they are not infinite, and the consequences for straying beyond them can be severe" (225). Such general notions of constraint and mobility must necessarily inform southern culture, but, because of the legacy of slavery and of *de jure* racial segregation, these territorial boundaries between racial cultures have traditionally had even greater repercussions for white and black southerners, who could at one time face legal consequences for traveling beyond the borders of their own culture and who can, even today, face social contempt for not staying within racial boundary lines.

A porch story told to me by Michael Cavanaugh on his back porch in Baton Rouge reflects how house porches can reinforce racial boundary lines. In our interview, Cavanaugh talked more of his grandparents' porch in Deridder, Louisiana, than of his own in Baton Rouge. His identity as a "porch person" goes back to times before air-conditioning, when the porch flourished in the South. This heyday of the porch in the twentieth century coincides with the era of legal racial segregation in the South. And the porch is necessarily implicated in governing racial boundaries that were firmly established in *Plessy v. Ferguson* in 1896 and not overturned in theory until *Brown v. Board of Education* in 1954 and in reality until the Civil Rights Act of 1964. Cavanaugh's grandparents' front porch was, as I have said, located in Deridder, a small town in central Louisiana, where racial divisions have been deeply felt throughout the years. Cavanaugh remembered the following story, indicating how the front and the back porches helped to sustain boundaries of race and class in the 1960s:

> Several times in my early childhood I can remember my family laying a body in state inside the house — what is the dining room — which is essentially a kind of common room. And the rest of us would be various places. I remember being just inside what they call "the hall" — that's just a big room inside the front door — when my Uncle Cavie was laying in state in the big room. That's when I was in the tenth grade, so this would be 1960. I glanced out, and I saw some black people walking up to the front door. Then I suddenly became aware that they had walked around. Well, pretty soon the story went through the whole house what had happened. My uncle had been the personnel director of the big paper mill in Elizabeth, Louisiana, that had a lot of labor trouble. He had navigated the trouble very well, and everybody loved him — which I

guess is what contributed to his heart attack at the age fifty—but these black people were from the mill. But they came around the back, and they asked some of the ladies in the kitchen, which is at the very back porch around the very end, if they would ask my grandmother, the matriarch of the family—my grandfather was long since dead—if they might be permitted to come in to pay their respects to the body.

Well, my grandmother was certainly not very liberal. In fact, she taught me two great, terrible little racial ditties: One was "I laid my gun upon the fence and there I pulled the trigger. Lam, bang, went the gun, and down came a nigger." The other saying she told all of us was "Treat 'em right, but not white." She was certainly no big racial liberal. But, she insisted—I guess it's just an element of what she understood being the hostess or the matriarch to be—that not only could they come in to see the body but a plate must be prepared for 'em—there were four or five as I recall—and, of course, there's tons of food anytime there's a funeral—and, so, they came in and saw the body and then went back to the back porch where they were given a huge plate. But nobody ever suggested anything other than them being on those back steps eating.

At the time, I remember thinking, you know, something's weird, you know, "what's wrong with this picture." But everybody, evidently, understood the rules. I didn't understand the rules of the culture, but I realized that if they wanted to pay their respects, it was supposed to not be denied them—be hospitable to them in terms of giving them food. But, they weren't to be seated at the table, or even on the front porches.

Michael Cavanaugh's candid story forcefully illustrates the complex policing of porch boundaries in a segregated South. On such a complicated transitional space, borders may not extend to the intimacy of the home's interior. In Cavanaugh's story, borders do not even extend to the front porch; in keeping with the larger ethos that endorsed white racial supremacy, the black workers had to eat their food on the back porch—in what Goffman calls the "back region"—to sustain the grandmother's notions of "southern decorum." The frightful "ditties" taught to Cavanaugh by his grandmother surely indicate why the front porch, a showcase for the community, was not available to the workers.

Cavanaugh's story proves that when southern porches are read in tandem with racial systems, they become inscrutable intersections that both connect and divide communities: Members of the Other race might gain access to the porch for the two cultures to come together and for relationships to spontaneously and temporarily flourish, but boundaries of racial separation—even now if one is lucky enough to have a porch with rockers meant for actual rocking—such boundaries may in some cases be established to limit conversation to the porch, to the *back* porch, or, for the true zealot, to no porch at all.

Jason Stagg, who grew up in central Louisiana, recounts the following story about a home rented by his parents while they built their own home:

> The owner of home always heard his grandmother tell the story of the white camellia bush. He says that members of the Knights of the White Camellia always planted a white camellia bush at the front of their home near the porch. This notified visitors of who the occupant of the house was and with whom they were associated. The Knights of the White Camellia were considered the "elite" group of leaders within the KKK. The time period that we are discussing here would be the 1920s and 1930s, especially during the Depression era. . . . Now, these are just stories passed down. I have no factual backing for them.

Whether true or not, the fact that the story has been passed down reminds us of the violence sometimes associated with racial segregation and the Ku Klux Klan. If members of the black community circulated this inside information about the white camellia bush, they certainly knew to keep their distance from this front porch.

Of course, the rules may not always be so punishing. The following story, told to me by Shannon Marquez McGuire, whose white family lived in the perhaps half-black Ninth Ward of New Orleans during the 1950s and 1960s, indicates how the porch can be used to increase interracial intimacy when the players are willing to resist institutionalized notions of decorum:

> When my family lived on Law Street in New Orleans, the neighborhood was isolated because it was a stretch of Law Street between two sets of railroad tracks. The neighborhood was nice and white up to the first railroad yard.

And then, you know, it turned black as soon as you literally crossed the tracks. There were about six pairs of tracks, so you had to really, really cross the tracks.

My little brother, Steve, was really shy. And Mrs. Ouida Goines, a black woman in the neighborhood, always had her apron on because she'd be working in her house, and she'd just come across the street to our store to do her shopping. My little brother would go get sweet potatoes and slip them in Mrs. Goines's apron pockets. And that meant, "Please bake me sweet potatoes." After meeting eyes with our mother on the other side of the counter, she would, winter or summer, take those sweet potatoes home and say, "Y'all come over in a few minutes." So we'd wash our hands and go over across the street, and she'd butter those sweet potatoes and put them in the oven. And in the summer, we would sit waiting out on the porch of her shotgun house and rock, or if it was cold, inside in her living room, and we'd ask her to tell us who all the pictures were.

In this quintessentially southern story, Shannon McGuire reveals how the porch can provide passage into the home of an Other. Her family, despite a meticulously groomed yard and a fairly prosperous family business, was considered to be "white trash," with their own "racial purity" occasionally questioned by other whites—for example, by some of the middle-class whites across ("really, really across") the six pairs of railroad tracks. Shannon McGuire's memory is, in many ways, her own counternarrative, one that resists the stereotypical labels that the "nice and white" neighborhood has assigned to the Other side of the tracks, labels which attach violence, laziness, and bigotry.

Indeed, in our academic, and even in our everyday, discussions of "whiteness," we too often tend to equate "white" with "privilege" without distinguishing class or gender or sexuality. But the white trash stereotype remains vital in American culture. As Matt Wray and Annalee Newitz, editors of White Trash: Race and Class in America, have so appropriately pointed out, " 'White trash' is not just a classist slur—it's also a racial epithet that marks out certain whites as a breed apart, a dysgenic race unto themselves" (1–2). And racial tensions between African Americans and poor whites have been legendary.

The porch in Shannon McGuire's story subverts our stereotypical notions of the hatred between poor whites and blacks in the South. Mrs. Goines's front porch allows instead for a celebration of the white children's relationship with their black neighbor, centered, appropriately, around the sweet potato, the "ur-food" for southerners, on the porch of a shotgun house, itself an African American architectural form.

We do not know from Shannon McGuire's story anything about Mrs. Goines's sense of place in the mostly black community or about her own understanding of her relationship with the white store owners. According to Shannon, Mrs. Goines was "a talented seamstress. Her house was one of the nicest doubles on the block." Shannon remembers her as "statuesque and always neatly dressed," someone whom Shannon's mother, Gloria Argus, "liked and respected." Shannon's story tells us that, whatever Mrs. Goines's own sense of the neighborhood was, she used her porch to bridge the cultural distance between herself and the only white children in her black neighborhood and took the extra step of inviting them indoors to view photographs of her family members.

New Orleans, as we have seen, is a much more creolized city than most. Would the same connections be apparent in other regions of the South? As I have made explicit from the beginning of this work, the parameters of my fieldwork have not allowed me to draw large generalizations about regional differences. I cannot say with assurance how a city different from New Orleans would use its porches. The stories would be as individual as the people who occupy the porches. But to briefly ask the question, while avoiding large generalizations, we can look at one fictional work. Dorothy Allison's *Bastard Out of Carolina* gives another look at "white trash" children who come upon black children on a South Carolina porch. Unlike the young Shannon McGuire, Bone Boatwright, the narrator of Allison's novel, has never really seen a black person up close, until her Aunt Alma moves into an apartment building with black neighbors during one of the many times she temporarily separates from her husband Wade. Such is not the typical housing arrangement in 1950s South Carolina. The Boatwrights are living at the time when the desegregation of American schools is being considered by the U.S. Supreme Court, a time when the white children in Bone's community have never seen black children up close. They do seem free, however, to use the word "nigger" in their speech and to taunt each other with the racial epithet. Perhaps her physical distance from black children makes her even freer to hurl the word. Bone tells the reader:

Setting Boundaries

People were crazy on the subject of color, I knew, and it was true that one or two of the cousins had kinky hair and took some teasing for it, enough that everyone was a little tender about it. . . . When I started school, one of the Yarboro cousins, a skinny rat-faced girl from the Methodist district, had called me a nigger after I pushed her away from the chair I'd taken for mine. She'd sworn I was as dark and wild as any child "born on the wrong side of the porch," which I took to be another way of calling me a bastard, so I poked her in the eye. (54–55)

The "skinny rat-faced girl" who taunts Bone for being a bastard—which in this novel is a metaphor for "white trash"—also uses the word "nigger" not just to establish Bone as a white person of another class, but also to degrade her with the racial epithet; she hurls the insult to establish Bone as what Newitz and Wray call a "dysgenic race." The "wrong side of the porch" is about more than being a "bastard." It is about being a "white trash bastard," a person "Othered" to the extent that she "isn't really white." Newitz and Wray mention that "the U.S. has an extremely impoverished political language of class," and, as a result, "whiteness is rarely connected to poverty in the U.S. imaginary" (8). The girl who insults Bone is using "nigger" metonymically to reveal her contempt for whites who dare not live up to middle-class standards. All this in spite of the fact that none of the children has ever really associated with people of other races.

Because people were "crazy on the subject of color," even though they had no real relationship with people of different races, it is no wonder then that when Bone, at the age of ten, sees from her Aunt Alma's porch black children at close range for the first time, she is curious about their appearance. She observes the children's dark skin, which, to her child's mind, looks like smooth chocolate and which places her cousin's white, pimply skin in relief. Bone studies the children from a distance, particularly the young girl who is not allowed to go outdoors. Bone can see the children only through a window. She describes the setting in the following words:

A long flight of steps ran off the porch and looped back past the lower apartment extending down to the yard. Grey and Little Earle were sitting on the top steps, leaning over to watch the kids from downstairs, who were looking out their windows up to where we all stood. Shiny brown faces kept pressing against the glass and then withdrawing, stern blank faces that we could barely tell one from the other.

"Niggers," Grey whispered proudly. "Scared of us." (83)

Grey gives voice to seemingly stereotypical racist views of the day, lending credence to the historical tension between poor whites and blacks; nevertheless, he ultimately winds up playing ball with the young boys who live near him. He is, for a moment, willing to step past his racist discourse and to allow the porch to be a cultural bridge, where a new relationship can temporarily flourish in this South Carolina community so deeply segregated that, unlike in New Orleans, white children can live ten years without ever seeing black children at close range. Despite the testing of racial boundaries, porch boundaries are maintained: Grey never goes into the black children's apartment.

Sindee Rippolo, who grew up in downtown Baton Rouge during the same period, echoes the pattern of using porches to build temporary bridges with set limits. In her porch memories, Rippolo demonstrates how racial boundaries in the city of Baton Rouge can be drawn (even still) in inscrutable ways, far more inscrutable than what we see in Bone Boatwright's segregated South Carolina territory. In fact, when my husband and I were shopping for a home to buy in Baton Rouge, we looked at a house on the north side of Government Street, but we were told by white folks that we "couldn't buy there." We could have bought on the south side—the "white" side—but the north side—the "black" side—was considered verboten. We eventually declined the house for structural reasons, but the lesson about boundaries in our capital city was enduring. Sindee Rippolo says:

We lived on 11th Street, which was all white people. On 12th Street one side was white, and one side was black. And on the same street maybe one block would be white and the next would be black. And then 13th Street was more black than white. . . . When we lived on another part of Government Street and South 13th Street, the kids across the street were black, and we were allowed to play with them, but we weren't allowed in one another's houses. But we could play with them. Really, I didn't understand why we couldn't go in their houses.

What the young Sindee did not understand was how the porch allows for a re-structuring of social norms. On it, relationships can temporarily thrive, even in a deeply segregated South. Consider the porch friendship of my grandmother, Florence Foreman, and her neighbor, Gloria Johnson.

TWO WOMEN AND A FRONT PORCH

My grandmother's neighbor of nearly twenty years, Gloria Johnson, moved from Massachusetts back to her home in Lake Charles, Louisiana, in 1964 after her husband died in an automobile accident. The year 1964 was, of course, a dramatic one in the racial history of America. In this year, we saw the passing of the federal Civil Rights Act, which contains provisions relevant to housing. Namely, Title VI bars discrimination in federally assisted programs, which in-clude mortgage-guaranteed housing accommodations.

Feeling her increased mobility through the enactment of civil rights legis-lation, Mrs. Johnson, a young widow in her mid-twenties with four children, bought into what she said was a "kinda classy area for the whites." The neighbor-hood, though clearly working class—with small frame houses dominating the landscape—also boasted, according to Mrs. Johnson, "paved streets and side-walks." In making such a move, Mrs. Johnson verified that minorities who have been discriminated against have often "found the acquisition of real property a reliable means of economic and social advancement" (Denton 3). And, to be sure, the single mother raised all of her children to success, even producing in her oldest daughter, Sandra, the first black woman to obtain a Ph.D. in engineering from Rice University.

During this changing racial context, my grandmother's porch became a site of limited racial interaction. Mrs. Johnson and other—usually female—neigh-bors often mounted the porch steps to cover typical domestic ground, discussing gardening, cooking, crocheting, and quilting. I said earlier that on my grand-mother's porch, our whiteness was very much perceived, marked, and named. My early understanding of this "shared-yet-separate" racial interaction with this black community motivated me to return to my grandmother's neighborhood—now entirely black—to interview Mrs. Johnson, who still lives in the house next to my grandmother's. From her I learned that my grandmother's porch was not only a woman's place; because it is situated between public and private spheres,

Gloria Johnson and her son Gregory, Lake Charles, La.
(Photograph by Jocelyn Hazelwood Donlon, 1995)

this porch also was able to become a "creolized space" where two cultures could come together to mix and mingle.

Today, when Mrs. Johnson talks of my grandmother, she does so with deep affection. And I believe this affection to be sincere. Both women were widows, both women prized their families above all else, and both women were interested in domestic activities. Mrs. Johnson was especially enthusiastic about my grandmother's extraordinary cooking. She said to me, "Miz Foreman, she used to make that chicken and dumplings. Which my son-in-law was talking about yesterday, about how his mother made chicken and dumplings. And I told him, 'Oh, this old white lady, she could *make* that chicken and dumplings.' She used to bring us some of that." Food *was* my grandmother's gift to others, a gift that Mrs. Johnson recognized, appreciated, and has made part of her own storytelling even today. Her conversation with me centered on other such domestic tasks valued by these two women. She talked about the routine daily activities that defined my grandmother's life as a southern woman — gardening, cooking, crocheting,

Setting Boundaries

quilting, and gossiping. And Mrs. Johnson learned about these activities by walking over to my grandmother's porch and visiting with her. As she said, "I went over there just about everyday. It used to be so nice and cool. And I would just go over there and talk with her." The two women, being widows, lived without an adult companion and worked at home. To counter not only their confinement to domestic roles but also their isolation from other adult company, they used the front porch as a social place. However, they rarely visited inside my grandmother's house. Nor was my grandmother a frequent guest in the homes of her neighbors—though Mrs. Johnson did talk of her delivering food to them, particularly when a relative had passed away. Mrs. Johnson told me that she would only occasionally go inside my grandmother's home, but she did not go inside for the purposes of "sitting and talking." As she said to me:

> I would always be on the porch. Miz Foreman loved the porch. She loved to be out there on the porch. And she would tell me a little gossip about white people . . . about the cemetery. You know, if they would have a funeral on Sunday, you'd have to pay extra, which I didn't know. Because I know years ago, the blacks, they would have funerals on Sunday all the time, but now, we don't have funerals on Sunday anymore. Now that's a night thing. We have funerals at night.

While the intensely segregated society around them was caught up in protecting separate worlds, these two women were more interested in learning of each other's culture by comparing and contrasting such things as their funeral practices. The subject of funerals was, without question, one of my grandmother's favorite topics and would be much appreciated by Mrs. Johnson, who participated in traditional African American burial practices that bestow great honor on those who have passed away.* It would have pleased my grandmother enormously that when she died, Mrs. Johnson and several other neighbors came to the

---

* Such African American customs no doubt have roots in African burial practices. African religions, which have shaped customs in the South, tend to stress the belief that one's life does not end with physical death; rather, death is a passage that allows for contact with the living. The ancestral community exists in African culture in the minds of the people living. Their "immortality" relies on their having a living family to honor and remember them. For further discussion, see John Mbiti's *African Religions and Philosophy*.

funeral home with a wreath whose banner read, simply, "The Neighbors." From their conversations on the porch, Mrs. Johnson learned of my grandmother's priorities, and, drawing from her own cultural practices, she honored them. But even though the porch allowed for such spontaneous gossip sessions for the two women to learn of each other's culture, the conversation did not cross the threshold to enter the private world of my grandmother's home.

I cannot claim to know with certainty the motivations for limiting conversation to the porch; the most detail I could get from Mrs. Johnson was that they stayed outside because of the weather. And, to be sure, their reasons may have been largely environmental: Louisiana's extended summers are miserably hot; Mrs. Johnson did not have a full front porch; and my grandmother enjoyed staying on her own front porch (she had only a tiny, tiny back porch) to perform her everyday domestic chores—snapping beans, crocheting, whipping up meringues. My grandmother's house was not air-conditioned—she defied the world around her by detesting air-conditioning, even trying to avoid homes that had it, as Mrs. Johnson's did. As a result of my grandmother's antipathy toward air-conditioning, conversation was more likely to occur on her own porch than inside her home or on someone else's porch.

I suspect, however, that there were traditional racial boundaries in operation that Mrs. Johnson was reluctant to acknowledge with me; in our interview, she was far more interested in celebrating my grandmother with me than in doing a social history of the South. Mrs. Johnson may even have been responding to my own whiteness, withholding some of her criticisms of my grandmother because of the cross-racial dynamic at work in our interview. I was perfectly aware in each cross-racial interview of cultural, emotional, and psychological baggage left by slavery and segregation in the South. Alert to the charges that the southern white majority has, in the words of David Goldfield, "fancied themselves as experts on Black behavior and feeling," while railing against "outsiders who presumed to divine the minds of Black Southerners from afar" (3), I undertook my cross-racial interviews with careful appreciation of how daunting the task was. I was mindful of Goldfield's charge that white people in the South too often only know a "stage Negro," who has been forced to heed the racial etiquette of the South. Goldfield describes the beginning stages of this etiquette, which has evolved in the post–civil rights era to a degree, as follows:

For Blacks encountering Whites, the code demanded . . . "sir" and "ma'am," averted eyes, preferably a smile, never imparting bad news, never discussing other Whites, and always exhibiting a demeanor that would make a White comfortable in believing that this deferential mien was not only right but the way things ought to be. The White, in turn, would almost always address the Black by a first name or by generic terms such as "boy," "uncle," or "aunty," regardless of age. The tone would always be condescending. And Whites enforced the code on others. (2–3)

As a result of such a code, which has reinforced the felt superiority of many whites, the two racial communities have — despite the established tradition of interracial communication — remained in many ways estranged. And in Goldfield's opinion, "White Southerners [have] effectively and ironically closed off the opportunity to know and benefit from their neighbors of three centuries" (4).

In my interview with Mrs. Johnson, I was sincerely interested in learning what racial boundaries she felt existed between her and my grandmother, but, for whatever reason, she was reluctant to go there. As I have said, though, I do suspect that racial boundaries were in operation in the porch relationship of the two women. I know, for example, that my mother remembered when homeless people roamed the South in search of food and shelter during the Great Depression. My grandmother's family, who lived in Moss Bluff during this period, often gave food to the "roadwalkers," as Shirley Ann Grau has termed them in her recent novel, but when black roadwalkers approached, they were directed to the back porch for their food, much like the African American workers in Michael Cavanaugh's story. The front porch was too public a space for such a transaction. Such a story confirms that my grandmother negotiated her generosity with food with an awareness of racial boundaries.

While I can only speculate as to the reasons for the women staying outdoors, I can say with more certainty that this story shows how my grandmother saw herself as the matriarch — and, by necessity, the white matriarch — of the neighborhood, who taught Mrs. Johnson more often than she was taught by her. She was about fifty years older than Mrs. Johnson and seemed occupied with instructing her in gardening, cooking, crocheting, and quilting. Most of Mrs. Johnson's stories were about what she learned from my grandmother. She even has a crocheting pattern that my grandmother gave her, which she showed me during the visit. And I believe that she was sincerely interested in learning from "this old white lady who could *make* those chicken and dumplings."

However, when I asked Mrs. Johnson, after listening to stories of how my grandmother had taught her so many things, if she had ever taught my grandmother anything, she laughed very heartily and tellingly and said, "NO, NO, NO, honey. She knew it all—she knew everything!" I could not help but hear the implied, "She was not one to be taught; she did the teaching," although Mrs. Johnson was far too kind to say that to my face, in part because of the deep respect within the African American community for the position of "grandmother." However, I remember my grandmother's stubborn pride, which undoubtedly was bound up in her racial identity. As Mrs. Johnson said, the neighborhood was a "kinda classy area for the whites," and my grandmother, I imagine, intended to keep it "kinda classy," by growing her legendary garden, feeding her hydrangea bushes with coffee grounds and rusty nails, and by turning her porch into a site not only for gossip, but also for domestic chores, for the instruction of the neighbors, and for the policing of children.

Mrs. Johnson's stories capture the essence of my grandmother. During their porch conversations, she got to know her well. Although they were not intimates, they were, nevertheless, on the liminal "space" of my grandmother's porch during this period of racial turbulence, able to negotiate institutionalized power relations—such as housing policies that do more segregating than integrating, such as notions of racial superiority and inferiority, or such as established gender roles which have historically limited women's roles to the home. They accomplished this negotiation despite their separate affiliations and despite any attempt on my grandmother's part to establish her own dominance within the neighborhood as the white matriarch. They were able to complicate this "white woman's place" by making it a hybrid, "creolized" space, one "betwixt and between absolute private and absolute public," a space where "relationships that would [have certainly been] impossible elsewhere" could not only flourish but endure (Beckham 75).

Today, the Lake Charles neighborhood is entirely black, and Gloria Johnson goes from porch to porch serving as the community matriarch. Perhaps she was my grandmother's porch companion because she sincerely valued, and continues to value, the role. Now she keeps watch over the children of Gwen Simeon, a young, single mother who lives in my grandmother's house. My grandmother would, I believe, be pleased. Gloria Johnson is now the neighborhood's matriarch, not unlike Rosie Lee Corley in her New Orleans neighborhood or Michael Cavanaugh's grandmother in hers. The porch, for these matriarchs, is indeed a "space" to assert their privilege in the community.

EXCLUSIVE PLACES OF PRIVILEGE

We have seen so far how porches can be "places" to assert class and race privilege, be it presumed, confirmed, or even invented. The status of the porch can be invented, even in childhood games, as illustrated by the following story by Lindsay Labanca, a young white woman from Metairie, a suburb of New Orleans:

> My parents, in their endless zeal for home improvements, painted the two porch columns rusty orange after a while. I still haven't forgiven them for that. See, the porch was a great place for games of Pretend because of those columns. They used to be ivory white, so my friend and I could imagine them to be the pillars of a Greek temple, or a palace hall, or a magician's lair. There just wasn't much we could imagine about them after they became orange. Also, my parents took out one of the columns, so the front porch looked really lopsided with only one column in front of the door. The porch was still nice to sit on, but we played more in my friend's house after that.

Obviously, the young Lindsay is not interested in turning her porch into a racially segregated site; she is interested in her games of "Pretend." What is noteworthy, though, is that in her games, her pillars are images of temples, palaces, or lairs. Her imagination, before the disgraceful painting of the columns, created a place of power. Her parents violated such playful constructions by disturbing the classical images of pillars in Lindsay's mind.

Other accounts of class power are more provocative. Sally Bradford Mauck of Columbus, Mississippi, recounted in a letter the following story, further proving that the porch is an everyday site of privilege. Mauck recalls the 1920s and 1930s in "a small town in the Mississippi Delta at Itta Bena near Greenwood." As the eighty-three-year-old Mauck tells it, "Most of the people in the town were land owners and well educated for the times. There was a very active social life, as well as church life there." When she talks about her porches, one can almost see the Old South come to life:

Setting Boundaries

Our house had a "morning porch" and an "afternoon porch." The morning porch was a screened, latticed and vine-covered place on the west side of the house. There in the mornings the women of the immediate neighborhood gathered for coffee after the men went to their various business affairs. There was a colored woman who lived with the family next door, who was greatly loved by all of us. Every morning she made the rounds of the immediate neighborhood (about ten houses) and then reported to the morning porch who was ailing and who needed attention and the general news of the families involved. Appropriate action was planned and taken to take care of whatever was needed. Then I remember school and church affairs were the topic of discussion. These sessions usually lasted about an hour, and then the women dispersed to their various homes.

The afternoon porch was on the east side of the house, and was a long, rambling, wide porch. Windows of the rooms were floor to ceiling with shutters. One end of the porch was rather secluded, shaded by shrubbery and trees. There was the usual rattan furniture there, and this particular spot was cooled by a ceiling fan. This was formal. In the late afternoon (turns were taken by the ladies of the social circle, which included all the maid families), tea was served with cut sandwiches or small cakes, and in the cool months sherry was served. The ladies dressed in their nice voile and linen dresses and wore hats and white gloves. The conversation here was also more formal. Most of these women belonged to what was called the "Delphian Club," which was a very comprehensive course of study in art, music, and literature. These topics formed the basis of conversation for these afternoon gatherings.

One item of conversation which stands out in my memory was the subject of where their children would go to college. There was never a question of whether they would go, just where. . . . Even when most of my contemporaries were thinking of college, the Great Depression had engulfed us. Our parents found ways to get us through. . . . Even though many could no longer attend the opera in New Orleans or travel as they had once done, they kept up with the newly published books, who was playing what concert where, and what great art collections were being shown. Looking back, I have a tremendous respect for the women who made a small rural town a place which encouraged one to know and enjoy those aspects of life which did not necessarily pay a wage.

Setting Boundaries

In a day when the agrarian South, indeed the entire country, was defined by economic privation, this informant lived a life of relative privilege. Markers of class privilege abound in this story: the hired maids during the Great Depression; black women who did the reporting to the local matriarchs; the "rattan furniture"; the tea with "cut sandwiches" or "small cakes"; the "linen dresses" and "white gloves"; and, of course, the attention to education, particularly a college education. The story leaves us to wonder whether the families of the maids who attended the gatherings also found the economic wherewithal to send their children to college.

I can certainly celebrate with this informant the sophisticated uses of porches in her small town. But because part of our work here is to be suspicious of nostalgic views of the porch, we should question what might have happened if a "white trash" woman had wanted to join in the literary discussions. What if, for example, Bone Boatwright, the young narrator in Dorothy Allison's *Bastard Out of Carolina*, had wanted to join the group of "ladies"? There is some evidence that she would have been welcome. The maids' families are included, after all. And certainly, the women here seem interested in the welfare of others who are in need. But perhaps she might have been excluded. And if she had, what might have occurred on those "morning" and "afternoon" porches? William Faulkner's *Absalom, Absalom!* begins to give us a clue as to what happens when "white trash," the "dysgenic race," knocks at the door of a "respectable" white family that doesn't crave the company of Others.

CLASS BOUNDARIES IN THE WORK OF WILLIAM FAULKNER

In Faulkner's novel of the Old South, the front porch is marked by class tensions: It is a controlled space that excludes Others on the basis of race and class, which come together in typically inscrutable ways. In *Absalom, Absalom!* it is a "white trash" boy who is spurned by a black slave. As the "skinny, rat-faced girl" in Allison's *Bastard Out of Carolina* demonstrated when she insulted Bone by calling her a "nigger," to be black in a segregated, racist society is typically considered, in the perverse scheme of things, to be "lower" than even the poorest white. When, in *Absalom, Absalom!*, the young Thomas Sutpen is, on the portico of the wealthy plantation owner, put in his "place" by a slave dressed better than he, he is being reminded that he is, in this instance, at the bottom of the social ladder. Indeed, as Eugene Genovese argues in his essay, " 'Rather Be a Nigger Than a Poor White Man': Slave Perceptions of Southern Yeomen and Poor Whites," slaves often derided poor whites because of their degraded and marginalized life.

Sutpen, on the plantation owner's portico, "never for one moment think[s] but what the [white] man would be as pleased to show him the balance of his things as the mountain man would have been to show the powder horn and bullet mold that went with the rifle" (286); however, the poor white boy gains an increased understanding not only of some differences between "black men and white men" but also of differences between "white men and white men" (282). He discovers that porches are border zones that symbolize economic, social, and racial authority; they can be "places" where those who possess the right combination of money, power, and privilege can assert control by admitting some and excluding others. The rich white man is not pleased to welcome Sutpen into his home to show him "the balance of his things." Labeled "white trash," the impoverished boy is instead snubbed by what he sees as a well-dressed slave. And the insult is compounded when he is told to avoid the portico altogether by entering through the back door on his next visit. On this portico, the boy comes face to face with pre–Civil War entanglements of race and class in the South, so that "Sutpen instantiates," as Hortense Spillers puts it, "the barefoot, bareass white boy who will spend his fictional career overcoming" (12).

It is obviously significant that Faulkner situates Sutpen's trauma on a "portico," which is literally a roofed porch supported by columns, with a pediment (or in Sutpen's case an impediment). As I discussed earlier, the portico, in its finest form, repeats classical architectural models, often signifying a house that belongs to an upper-class family. In Faulkner's novel, on the portico of white wealth, Sutpen reaffirms his commitment to gaining a porch of his own that will symbolize the reach of the wealth and power he intends to accumulate. After building his conspicuous plantation in Jefferson, Mississippi, with a captive French architect and naked slaves, Sutpen will, like the rich plantation owner, instruct his own slaves to regulate the flow of people in the porch, compelling them to reinforce the very power that oppresses them. Sutpen will emulate the patriarch by not only spending his afternoons in "barrel stave hammocks between two trees" (284) but also by barring the likes of Wash Jones from his door, as well as excluding his own racially mixed son, Bon, from his home. Sutpen indeed seems intent on pursuing the same exclusive, intolerant course as the rich white plantation owner. But because of his faulty "design," he ultimately must bear witness to his home's decay.

Porches, as this chapter has shown, are frequently about overcoming the power of others, about converting community "places" into "spaces" in a South that has historically been characterized by its racial and class divisions, divisions that take a variety of forms depending on the cultural, and even geographical, circumstances. Certainly generational and gender norms will also affect how power struggles get played out on the porch.

Earlier we read a story by Lillie Petit Gallagher, who grew up along Bayou Lafourche in South Louisiana during the 1940s. In Chapter 2, Gallagher recounted her childhood memories from Cut Off, Louisiana, and depicted the labor of an oyster lugger viewed from the front porch, the daily chores accomplished on the back porch, and the different forms of work and leisure on the various house porches at different times of the day, from gutting fish in the morning to crocheting doilies in the late afternoon. I admit here that I saved Gallagher's final paragraph to introduce this chapter on family dynamics — dynamics grounded largely in gender and generational differences. In the final paragraph of her letter, Gallagher writes:

> In the mornings it was the back porches that were the bustling places of enterprise necessary to maintain the family household. But in the mid and late afternoons, it was clearly the front porch that was the *Queen of Space* [emphasis added]. Only when the mosquitoes became too fierce would someone reluctantly announce, "Allons rentrer, les mostiques va nous enlever" [let's go in, the mosquitoes will carry us away]. On the front porch, another day had come to a close.

I delayed the conclusion of Gallagher's narrative because of her fortuitous phrase, "Queen of Space." In light of our continued use of de Certeau's distinction between "space" and "place," Lillie Gallagher's choice of the word "space" is noteworthy. Indeed, the individuals on this porch in Cut Off, Louisiana, are actively engaged in the creation of a Cajun identity that is tied closely to fisheries and wildlife. Geography is central here: Only from porches along bayous and waterways can the "cycle of a watery harvest" be witnessed, in this case from Cut Off to New Orleans and back again. And in few communities outside South Louisiana would Cajun French be used to call the family indoors, away from the mosquitoes.

Gallagher says elsewhere, "In Cut Off, along the west side of Bayou Lafourche, the houses were all oriented toward the east. Front porches were ideal spots for socializing and relaxing in the cool of an afternoon." The physical geography of this region levies pressure on how the ethnic community will make use of its porches. The houses stretched "single file, along the bank of the bayou." But the neighbors were willing to walk the necessary distance along those banks, on their way, as Gallagher tells it, "to the church, to the store, to the school ferry, to the picture show, to the dance hall, to the restaurant, to the feed store and to the local cafe . . . all along the way stopping to visit with whoever, for the moment, was sitting on the front porch." The neighbors were willing to go the distance to sustain their community identity, from sharing conversations in the French language specific to them, to dancing at the dance hall, to preparing foods that one can find only in South Louisiana.

More important for our purposes here is that Lillie Gallagher, perhaps unintentionally, feminizes the front porch, calling it the "*Queen of Space.*" Perhaps she sees the porch as a feminine space because her vision of it is associated with socializing, and in the South, as elsewhere, women are typically the guardians of social life—the ones who will keep conversation flowing, sometimes seemingly at *any* price. Indeed, in nearly all of the stories we have heard so far, the women have been the bearers of community news. But whatever Gallagher's motivation, her phrase invites our attention to the porch as a gendered space. And because the porch was more central to family life before the advent of air-conditioning and before women began to leave the home to work, the stories in this chapter will focus on what I have continued to call the porch's heyday of the twentieth century—from the early part of the 1900s to the late 1960s and early 1970s.

In this discussion, I do not intend "gender" to be synonymous with "feminine" or even "feminism." I use the term to determine the ways in which porch activities are constructed as either "masculine" or "feminine" or as a negotiation of both gendered positions. The manifestations of these gendered activities can vary from performance to performance. Though the traditional porch is certainly framed in femininity, we will nevertheless see that, even during the pre-1970 years in which we tend to categorize the public world as "male" and the domestic world as "female," the porch cannot always be slotted into neatly gendered categories.

In her collection of essays *Space, Place, and Gender*, Doreen Massey, a British geographer, makes the following claim: "Space and place, spaces and places, and our senses of them (and such related things as our degrees of mobility) are gendered through and through. Moreover they are gendered in a myriad different ways, which vary between cultures and over time. And this gendering of space and place both reflects *and has effects back on* the ways in which gender is constructed and understood in the societies in which we live" (186). If "places and spaces" are gendered in "myriad different ways," if they are marked as belonging either to men or to women or to both, certainly the porch bears such markings. And if these markings "vary between cultures and over time," then the norms of different southern cultures will influence how these spaces are gendered. Most of the following examples, again, come from the early part of the twentieth century to the late 1960s and early 1970s, when southern families typically made daily use of house porches, so the norms of an agrarian South will influence much of the gendered activity.

It is tempting to call the porch a "woman's space" simply because southern women have traditionally been the "keepers of the house," and, thus, guardians of the porch. Such views of women as the "angel of the house" are typically romanticized in terms of family stability. As Massey says:

> The construction of "home" as a woman's place has carried through into those views of place itself as a source of stability, reliability and authenticity. Such views of place, which reverberate with nostalgia for something lost, are coded female. Home is where the heart is (if you happen to have the spatial mobility to have left) and where the woman (mother, lover-to-whom-you-will-one-day-return) is also. . . . The identities of "woman" and of the "home-place" are intimately tied up with each other. (180)

Perhaps Gallagher crowned the porch as "Queen" because she was writing in a nostalgic tone about bygone homelife, and, as Massey has said, the identities of our "home-places" are interwoven with our conceptions of "woman." Moreover, most of the informants who have been interested enough in celebrating their memories of "home porches" to participate in my project have been women, though certainly not all.

I will acknowledge that when I began my research for this project, I first conceived of the porch as woman's territory, primarily because of my early association with my grandmother's porch. My grandfather died when I was only six years old, and he was bedridden with emphysema for many years before he died. I rarely saw him out of his bed, much less out of his house. And my mother told me that she did not remember her father sitting on the porch very often, even in his healthier days. He preferred to be indoors where he could more easily listen to his radio.

There are other reasons why my early formations of the porch were feminized. In traditional conceptions of the porch, we typically think of domestic assignments as being charged to women, largely because women's mobility (particularly middle-class, white women's mobility), until the last two decades, was usually limited to home. In most of the stories we have heard from informants so far — stories that often represent an agrarian South before the women's movement — it has been the women who have snapped beans, peeled potatoes, desilvered corn, stitched together quilt pieces, and crocheted doilies on front and back porches. If the porch is a liminal space, situated between the private world of the family and the public world of the community, the direction of the porch, for women, often leads back to the home's interior, the domestic sphere.

This is not to say that the porch does not connect women with the outside community. Women *have* used the porch to feel tied to the outside world, particularly in the practice of everyday gossip. In making this generalization, I do not mean to say that only women gossip. And I *certainly* do not mean to say that gossip is always malicious. As Patricia Meyer Spacks says in her book *Gossip,* "In practice, the gossip that seeks to damage others is probably relatively rare — easy to imagine as an activity of the faceless figures who inhabit dark recesses of our minds, but infrequently evident in our living rooms" (4–5). Malicious gossip on the porch, because of the porch's public nature, would be even less likely. Gossip is a conversational activity traditionally *constructed* as female. The role of women in the community and the very nature of the porch, which is "betwixt and between" public and private, come together to produce a form of gossip that operates as an "instrument of social control" (Spacks x).

PORCH GOSSIP

The following stories recount events from the 1930s to the 1970s, events that represent the porch as a traditional site for women's gossip. These stories range from representing gossip as benign facts about others to portraying gossip as "an instrument of social control." Consider the following story written by Nina W. Jones for the East Baton Rouge Council on Aging's publication, *Platinum Record*: "With no air conditioning, the houses [in our neighborhood] had screen doors. And while sitting in the swing, I could smell the odors from neighborhood houses and know what they were having for supper. Mother always sat in the swing mid-morning waiting for the mailman, and then after supper we sat there to watch anything that might occur in the neighborhood" (17). The knowledge of and conversation about others in this community seem harmless enough: Nina Jones's family can detect what's cooking for supper in the neighborhood, and the mother seems to watch the community's goings-on with the benign motivation of simply passing the time. This mother and daughter appear to spend much of their time watching, listening, and even smelling simply to know what's going on in the neighborhood. In doing so, they are once again conforming to southern norms that stress the connection of family to community.

Lillie Petit Gallagher's story depicts a family with more of a stake in the life of the community. In the following example, gossip is almost a form of social inquiry, reflecting the family's awareness of the work world that surrounds and influences their own:

> One could quickly learn what was going on in the community by simply "setting a spell" on the front porch. In the mid-afternoon of one day, Mr. Melancon passed with his old "pick up" filled with sacks of potatoes. In the mid-afternoon of the next day, Mr. Melancon passed back, his potatoes having been replaced with chickens, each with one foot tied with a string to a brick in his flat bed. Squawking chickens in Mr. Melancon's pick up, a sure sign that he had been to the French market in New Orleans. You could go tell your mama.

Such benign gossip actually enables the women and children in 1940s Cut Off, Louisiana, to track the economic life of the "Mr. Melancons" in their community.

C. Jean Jackson's example is even more localized in its concern but socially significant, nonetheless. Her mother gossips about specific members of the community, but in no way does she seem malicious; she is simply staying abreast of the events in her neighbors' lives in order to feel connected with them: "Mother would sit out there and wave to the people passing by. Mother would say, 'There

Shaping the Family

go the Turners. I see they have the grandkids with them. They're probably going to spend the week. Their son-in-law must be going to Memphis to see about that job.' Or, 'I see the McVeys had the Preacher for dinner today.' We seldom saw a stranger." "Gossip" such as this keeps a neighborhood from becoming estranged. And here, as is often the case, it is the woman of the house who is guardian of the social life of the porch, using it to keep the family connected to the community.

In Chapter 2, we heard from Kate Daniels, who grew up in Richmond, Virginia, and whose storytelling history on her paternal grandmother's porch informed her essay, "Porch-Sitting and Southern Poetry." Daniels also talks explicitly about some of the gossip told to her:

As [my grandmother] gave me her versions of the lives that surrounded us on Royal Avenue, the xenophobic egoism of early childhood was punctured pleasantly for me, and I became aware that life itself is ultimately kind of a story: The people whose lives she recounted to me—the Thompsons, who lived in a secretive and possibly violent world in their large, unpainted house three doors away; the sad and beaten-down Joneses, who had lost their only son, Sparky, my father's best friend, in the Korean War; the Reverend Holloway, a Christian Science minister, and his family, who lived across the street and seemed very provincial to us, with their plain clothes, their flat and tidy hairdos, and the fact that they didn't own a television set—all these exercised an endless and perambulating fascination on my growing mind and fancy. (62)

As Kate Daniels realizes, gossip is a social narrative, in this case for the women in the family, and gossip as such fires the imagination to speculate about the private, "possibly violent," world that lives beyond the threshold.

Liz Kraemer of Vacherie, Louisiana, gives us the most explicit example of how gossip can move from the mundane to the regulatory:

Although, during the late forties and early fifties the houses were equipped with window fans or attic fans which pulled in the outside air, we still preferred to join the neighbors on the front porch after the supper dishes were washed and the kitchen was cleaned. The gathering was not always on the same front porch. . . . Heaven forbid that anyone should commit a "faux pas." If the offender was a member of the group, he/she was corrected in no uncertain terms. If not a member of the group, the "faux pas" was discussed with a sense of disapproval, but was gossip, no less. (Speaking of "faux pas," the entire conversations were in French.) The sense of disapproval caused the young to realize that in order to be accepted by the community, one had to lead a virtuous life.

Gossip in this Cajun neighborhood keeps the community members on the straight and narrow path. And in this way gossip again becomes gendered as female, because in this social context, it would have been the mothers in the neighborhood charged with the shaping of "a virtuous life." These maternal responsibilities would be modified and shaped in part by community gossip shared on the front porch, the "front region" as Goffman called it, which was central to the impressions that a family and a community wanted to communicate.

But even as the women in these stories use front porch gossip to shape their notions and impressions of family and community, they must negotiate their individual desires with the demands of the physical space itself. In other words, the liminality of the porch modifies the kind of gossip women can participate in. On the porch, nothing should be said that cannot be overheard or taken up by passersby. The social conditions are far too risky to allow for the kind of gossip that is a private, confidential conversation between two people. Porch gossip, particularly gossip shared on the "front region" of the house, is not necessarily intimate. It is more like a drama. Patricia Meyer Spacks describes this kind of gossip as people "speaking the language of shared experience, revealing themselves as they talk of others, constructing a joint narrative—a narrative that conjures up yet other actors, offstage, playing out their own private dramas" (3). Spacks insists that this kind of gossip can be shared by no more than three people, and preferably two. Otherwise, the conversation produced is only a "simulacrum" of gossip (4).

If porch gossip is only a "simulacrum" when five or six people share it rather than two or three, then so be it. The more important point here is that the porch itself has rendered gossip a "simulacrum." Few people aware of the rules of southern conversation would risk—particularly on the front porch, which is subject to spontaneous visitors—the discussion of topics deemed too intimate, too private, or too grievous for the public world to hear. Individuals would likely cross the threshold for such private talk. Some might even switch languages, if they could. Eugene Walter, whose essay "Secrets of a Southern Porch" was mentioned earlier, recalls in the same essay his grandmother's strategic use of French in her porch gossip in Mobile, Alabama: "At night, porch life went on forever. When the gossip got really good, my grandmother would switch from English to French, so that little eavesdroppers couldn't hear: 'And nobody knew where she was, they looked high and low, nobody could find her, and then she was seen in New Orleans with—' And the rest would be in French" (63). As we saw earlier, children are sometimes included in the community gossip, but they are often relegated to a position of eavesdropping. Indeed, when talking about the porch during its heyday as a space for women, it is nearly impossible to separate the activities of the women from the activities of the community children. The stories that follow look at how the porch has traditionally been used by neighborhood mothers to keep children under control.

GUARDING THE CHILDREN

I mentioned previously how my grandmother, long after her own children had left home, policed the children of her neighborhood. Often, she reported back to the parents when youngsters had strayed beyond their designated limits—using community gossip to keep children in line. But gossip gained from the porch and used to control children is not the only way the porch functions in mothers'—and grandmothers'—rearing of children. Sindee Rippolo, who talked earlier about the inscrutable racial boundaries of her porch in 1950s Baton Rouge, also talked about how her grandmother used her porch to control the young Sindee and her sisters when they went to stay with her:

> We would go spend the day with [my grandmother], and we were not allowed to get off that front porch; it was like a prison wall around it. Her neighbor's children would sit on their front porch, and we would talk to one another; we weren't even allowed to go play. So my sisters and I would always laugh about how we used to sit on my grandmother's front porch and all we could do was talk to the little kids next door. We couldn't go play with them; we couldn't get out of her sight.

When Rippolo first began telling her story to me, I assumed that the grandmother had created prison walls around her porch simply to ensure her grandchildren's safety. But as our conversation continued, I realized that the prison walls were constructed as a response to the grandmother's perceived differences in social class. As Rippolo tells us:

> When I went to visit my grandmother, there was nothing wrong with the kids in her neighborhood. She just didn't want us visiting with them, crossing that porch line. My grandmother was originally from New Orleans, and she never got over the fact that she had to leave New Orleans and live where my mother was. It was a big transition for them. She made a life out it, but she always had that aristocratic way about her from living in New Orleans. She never did feel that these people [in her neighborhood] were up to her class. My mother's people before the stock market crash owned a macaroni factory in New Orleans, so they were used to having money and servants and all. And when they lost everything in the crash they had to go out and work. That was a whole different type of thing; my grandfather never had to work before that happened. And then they had to come here and live in rented houses and those kinds of things. It just came and went with us — part of living.

Sindee Rippolo's narrative reminds us that rearing children is tied not only to issues of gender and generation, but also to class constraints. This is not a porch grounded in the cultural norms of an agrarian South; it is, rather, a place where "aristocratic," urban values are privileged — even if the grandmother must enforce these values in her working-class neighborhood so strongly that the children sense a "prison wall" surrounding them.

Some mothers have even used the porch to punish children, as the following story by Renee Coleman Daigle illustrates. The young Renee often visited her grandparents' house in rural Brookhaven, Mississippi: "At my Granny's house, I remember us always being out on the porch. Children were even punished on the porch. The punishment was that you had to sit on the bench on the porch. And everybody else could play. They'd be playing in the dirt while we were in 'time out.' My cousin, Buddy, he was always punished on the porch." The least comfortable piece of furniture — the bench — becomes the household brig for Buddy and sometimes for Renee. The children are placed in "liminal confinement," able to view the goings-on of the other children but unable to join in with them. Betwixt and between isolation and participation, the children here feel a special kind of punishment on their grandmother's porch, where they are forced to watch from the bench the fun they are missing.

Lynn Veach Sadler, who grew up "in The Friendship community (as it still must be deemed), west of Goshen Swamp and southwest of Rooty Branch Church and Summerlin's Crossroads, south of Beautancus, southeast of Faison, east of Bowdens, and northeast of Warsaw and Magnolia in North Carolina," has written an essay, "Of Swings Deaf and Mute but Not Dumb," in which she recalls generational and gender dynamics of the porch swing she grew up with. She says, "The swing was tacitly reserved for the matriarch or oldest woman present," which meant her "Grannie," in spite of the porch's literally belonging to Lynn Sadler's mother (2). When her Grannie would eventually invite the young Lynn to sit with her on the swing, the invitation was not without complications:

After Grannie had held sway in the swing for some requisite length of time, she would invite me to join her. Now, I loved Mama, Grannie, and the swing, and this invitation to swing was an early approach-avoidance conflict for me. *Not to swing* was to deny Grannie's pull and my own delight in swinging gently beside her. *To swing* birthed a certain coolness in my mother until long after Grannie and her current husband had departed. . . . The "old Veach house" had come to Grannie through her second husband, whose children by his first wife were, accordingly, eternally aggrieved. In turn, Grannie gave her home to my father, her one surviving child by "Mr. Veach," as I always heard my grandfather referred to. Grannie, however, relentlessly maintained giver's rights and found countless ways to remind my mother of her mother-in-law's largess. Mama added the swing; Grannie appropriated it.

Grannie, I have since realized, used the swing as a "bully pulpit." It automatically conveyed status to its occupants, and she punctuated her pronouncements with a forward thrust. On the one hand, when my mother was speaking, Grannie would force the swing back and hold it in place. It took me a while to learn swing grammar/body language, and, once I had and was no longer so attentive as I ought to have been, Grannie would pinch me on the knee to get my attention and make me re-join her rhythm. I did know better than to react to her gentle pinches out loud. (2–3)

The young Lynn is being drawn into the competitive pressures existing between her mother and grandmother. Hers was a tricky endeavor: to defer to both elders without offending either one, to read and respect the grammar and body language of the swing, and, most important, to secure some pleasure for herself.

Some grandmothers can make their proprietary notions less subtle to their grandchildren. Emily Fontenot from Eunice, Louisiana, reveals in the following story the turf conflict on her grandmother's porch:

Ever since I was in kindergarten, I would ride the bus home from school. It never failed that I would see my grandmother rocking and waiting for all of her grandkids—except on rainy days. We would all run off the bus to give her kisses then throw our books inside and play on the porch. Well, about an hour later, Mrs. Betty from across the street would walk over. This was our signal to get lost. Mom (what we called my grandmother) would just say, "Okay, kids, go play in the back," and we would run to the back. And each day she and Mrs. Betty would drink a cup of coffee and talk for about an hour. I always thought that was so neat. It was like the porch was "their turf," and everyone knew it. . . . The thing that I find so interesting is that, to this day, anyone can find those two sitting on the swing on my grandmother's front porch at 4:00 P.M. Mrs. Betty's husband is still alive, and my grandmother lives alone. But my little brother rides the bus to her house now after school. He actually said to me laughing one day, "Man, Emily, Mom and Mrs. Betty are going to rot on that front porch. They sit there every day. Was it always that way?" I simply told him, "Ever since I can remember."

At times, grandmothers will attempt to erase some of the age-related boundaries and become children again with their grandchildren. Amie McWhorter remembers discovering the playful, childish natures of her great-aunt and grandmother:

This past summer, we were at a family reunion in Alabama. We were sitting on the porch listening to my Great Aunt Rea tell stories about when she and my grandmother were young. My Great Aunt Rea is 82 years old, and my grandmother is now 77. They began to talk about this thing they did as children, this "bear walk," where they would walk on all fours, with the legs and arms both straight. They started to talk about how they were the only ones who could do it because they were so short (they're both under 4'11"). All of us grandchildren were about to die laughing when my great-aunt and my grandmother started to do the bear walk. There we were, watching an 82-year-old and a 77-year-old walking on all fours on the porch in front of the whole family. They began to wonder if anyone else in the family could do it, so they asked me since I am the shortest of the grandchildren. To their surprise and mine, I could do it!

If the porch can level the playing field, so to speak, it can also invert power relations. The following story by Ottie Hazlewood Mercer illustrates how children can manipulate the porch to their advantage. My Aunt Ottie's story is set in the late 1930s on the family farm in Opelousas, Louisiana:

> I must've been about six years old, and I was told that it was time to take a bath. Apparently, I didn't want to stop playing, or something. So I went the other way, and Mama came after me. Well, I ran, and she ran. I beat her to the front porch and started down the steps, just about the time that she got to the edge of the porch. And she grabbed my hand to pull me and stop me. And she pulled my arm out of its socket. And so she spent the rest of the day rocking me with my arm on a pillow after they put it back in place.

On this porch space, between the world of play (which to children means perceived freedom) and the world of parental authority (which has little to do with play), Aunt Ottie tussles with her mother, struggling to assert her own authority. And if my grandmother, Annie Seales Hazlewood, was the temporary victor, she certainly paid for it in the end. In fact, on the day that Aunt Ottie told this story to me and to other women in my extended family, my own mother's response was, "She must've rocked you for days, as tender-hearted as she was!" The porch in previous stories might have been a "place" for mothers and grandmothers to feel and declare their power, but the porch rocker, in Aunt Ottie's story, becomes a "space" for reconciliation, where mothers, especially "tender-hearted" ones, can offset their occasional stepping over the line in their daily tasks of guarding and controlling children.

Thus, the porch is certainly not always a site of freedom for children, despite our collective tendency to romanticize it, even today, as a site of game playing. And this theme of generational conflict is echoed in other stories. For example, Emma H. Major from Baton Rouge speculates about the social controls made possible by the front porch during her own youth in the 1930s: "Was all this visible, open-air activity tantamount to living in a gold-fish bowl? Was it a prime example of 'invasion of privacy'? Somehow, we never thought of it that way. Behavior, I'm sure, was modified by what the neighbors might think. Little children behaved themselves because they never knew when someone's mother might be watching! Front porch behavior was mostly polite behavior." Notice that, in her description of the "gold-fish bowl" nature of the porch, Emma Major says "someone's mother," not "someone's father," might be watching. Major reinforces our notions that it is the mothers who mostly use the porch to shape the behavior of their families. In all of the above stories, it is the domestic power of women that controls the children's behavior, even, at times, turning porches into a "prison wall." These mothers and grandmothers have demonstrated that in guarding the children, they have the potential to turn the porch into a "place" of parental authority. But this doesn't mean that children cannot occasionally turn the porch to their own advantage.

MAKING A "SPACE" FOR CHILDREN

As we have already seen, children have occasionally felt free to manipulate the authority of adults on the porch, seeking to create their own "space" in which to confront their parents. Children can also make creative use of porch spaces in their invention of porch games. We read earlier of the shadow play with headlights created by the three sisters from Mississippi. Rose Anne St. Romain offers an additional example here, telling of how the eight children in her family, along with other children in the small central Louisiana town of Mansura, used to play a game called "shoes" on the porch swing:

When we were kids, we played this wonderful game on the front porch. It was called "shoes." And about . . . well as many people could play it at one time as you could fit on the front porch swing. 'Cause we had a swing. We still have the same swing on the front porch. And this is how you played it. We would all get on the swing, and you'd get that swing going as fast as you could. Then when it was going real high, you'd take off your shoes, and at random you'd throw your shoes down—everybody would throw their shoes down—the shoes would be scattered all over the porch. And then you'd get the swing going again because you'd lost some momentum. And you'd get that swing going. And on the count of "GO," everybody on the swing had to lean over and pick up as many shoes as they could and put 'em in their lap. And you had to be careful because the person next to you might snatch your shoes, or the shoes might fall back on the ground or slip out the back. And whoever collected the most shoes won. And that's how we played "shoes." I don't remember ever being taught to play shoes, but I do remember waiting to be old enough to play.

When I asked Rose Anne if the children ever fell out of the swing, she said, "Of course we fell out of the swing! But the worst thing was when the chain would break in the middle of shoes. Then you could break kids." The wild abandon of these children, unaware of any conceivable dangers involved in their invented game, explains largely just why parents were forced to police them. And even in this game, the children had to wait to be old enough to play. Nevertheless, in their moments of what appeared to be total freedom, they were able—sometimes too literally—to break the chains of adult supervision. But the parents could feel relatively safe that the children were not in too much danger. After all, other mothers were watching.

Frances Stirling, who grew up in Baton Rouge during the 1940s and 1950s, writes of her childhood games, grounded largely in her and her siblings' imaginative powers:

When my sisters and I were very young, we spent countless hours on the porch, building everything imaginable with brick blocks or clay, designing clothes for our paper dolls, making up new rules for our board games, inventing secret clubs and playing with our Cocker Spaniel, Ginger Lady. Sometimes we would adjust the chains on the swing to move it as high as possible to make a time machine. We traveled all over the world in that ship and had fantastic adventures. Occasionally we would get together with neighbors and tell ghost stories. Shadows loomed menacingly, the night grew uncomfortably cool, and chills ran up and down our spines.

And my sister, Karen Hazelwood Duplantis, who is nine years older than I and has memories of MaMaw Hazlewood that I don't share, told me the following story:

When I was about ten years of age, my daddy's mother, MaMaw, remarried after being a widow for many years. Her new husband, "Papa Beall," had a large home in the country outside of Opelousas. This house had a very large front porch with a swing at each end. This was a new experience for me because my other grandmother, Mama's mother, only had one swing on her porch. Although we knew we'd get in trouble, my brothers and cousins would get in each swing and swing as hard as we could trying to touch our toes together. There was no way we could swing that close together but each time we'd go higher and keep trying. Maybe as children, we felt if we could touch toes, we would always have someone close even if we would get in trouble trying.

While children have sometimes been satisfied to use the porch merely for play, adventure, and for an occasional frisson, they have sometimes used the porch to put adults in their "place," giving them their "come uppings." Consider the following example told by Brother Joe Bartlett, a Southern Baptist minister from Lake Charles, Louisiana (the same Joe Bartlett who ordained my father, who married my parents, and who buried my mother). "Bro Joe," who is now nearing the age of ninety, was a frequent visitor on my grandmother's porch in Lake Charles. He was pastor of Calvary Baptist Church when my father was assistant pastor. During their working together in the mid-1940s, the young ministers ate more than one Sunday dinner (meaning midday meal) at my grandmother's table. Bro Joe, in his stentorian, ministerial tones, recently told me the following story:

Miz Foreman had some neighbors—we all were neighbors, we all went to old Calvary Church. One Sunday we had dinner at Miz Foreman's, and after dinner we sat on the porch to enjoy our coffee. There was a little neighbor boy by the name of Bernard, on the left of the house. And this little fella was learning to ride a tricycle on the sidewalk out there. So he got his tricycle, and he'd riiide up and down, past about two houses—his house and the Foreman house. And he'd try to turn that tricycle around, but he'd drop the back wheels of that tricycle off the sidewalk, and he couldn't stand it back up. So he'd start yelling for somebody to come and help him.

Apparently we were a little bit slow in leaving our coffee to go help that kid ride his tricycle. So right in front of the Foreman house he fell off the sidewalk, the back wheels did, and he was whooping and yelling to try to get somebody to come help him. His mama and daddy lived next door, and they were listening, too. They hadn't moved.

So he decided that he'd pay us all a compliment. He couldn't get the hang of it, so he just took his hand, waved it over us like a preacher, and said, "Alla y'all are just nothin' but a bunch of sumbitches."

Shaping the Family

The child here seems to understand perfectly well the full weight of his malediction. Perhaps he felt free to curse his elders because his parents were not present. Perhaps he felt at liberty because the adults on the porch could not easily catch him or seemed disinclined to do so. Perhaps it was the public nature of the porch that allowed him to show his anger with the uncooperative adults, who made a public spectacle of his clumsy efforts. Perhaps he was just a disrespectful brat. Whatever his motivation, the adults on this porch were certainly put in their place.

In truth, though, children are rarely the victors. The following poignant story demonstrates how adults can wield their power over the young. Because of the sensitive nature of the story, I have changed the names of the major characters and deleted the storyteller's name:

Uncle Beau and Aunt Chantelle lived close to my parents. When my cousins would come in from out of town, sometimes we would go visit Aunt Chantelle and Uncle Beau. Not because they were particularly interesting, but because it was the right thing to do. Somehow it was communicated to us to go see Uncle Beau and Aunt Chantelle—only if they were on the porch. If they weren't on the porch, we didn't have to go. But if we were playing in the yard, and they were on the porch, we knew we should go over and tell them hello.

I have two girl cousins, Sharon and Grace, they're sisters. Sharon is six or eight months older than me, and Grace is six or eight months younger than me. So we were kind of a threesome. And Sharon and I were always slender when we were little. Grace was not. Grace was always chubby. Always. And when we would go to see Aunt Chantelle and Uncle Beau, we would kiss Aunt Chantelle and we would kiss Uncle Beau, and, invariably, Uncle Beau would say to me and to Sharon, "Well it's so good to see you, blah, blah, blah, you look so pretty today!" And then he'd look at Grace and then he'd say, "You're improving." Even as a little girl, I remember feeling so sorry for Grace. It quickly got to where Grace didn't want to go see Aunt Chantelle and Uncle Beau. But she always went because that was "the right thing to do."

The porch here imposes lamentable notions of social decorum on the young Grace. She is *compelled* by family norms to socialize, only to face her own humiliation. (I am reminded here of the black people who went to pay their respects to Michael Cavanaugh's uncle, knowing they would be ushered to the back porch.)

Nevertheless, Grace capitulated because it was "the right thing to do." Fortunately for the young Grace, the porch provided an easy escape. One wonders, in fact, if the uncle in this story would have been so thoughtless had the young girl visited him inside his own home. It is not hard to believe that he would. But perhaps because the porch, in its liminality, temporarily redefines social relations, he felt more at liberty to tease the child about her appearance, aware that her visit was temporary and that she had an easy escape—though such an interpretation certainly gives him the benefit of the doubt.

We are beginning to see that the porch is not merely a "woman's space," as Uncle Beau painfully illustrates and even as Bro Joe, labeled a "sumbitch" by the young Bernard, reveals. It is not just a post where neighborhood mothers can do their patrolling of children or accomplish their daily chores and gossip. We have gradually transitioned from the feminine side of the porch to see how men, also, use it to exercise power and individuality.

Such a claim could make us automatically assume that the porch is a "place" framed in patriarchal power. And to some degree this is true. As we saw in Chapter 2, Hurston's uses of the porch in *Their Eyes Were Watching God* certainly bear out such a claim. Janie Crawford is compelled to reshape the terms of her husband's porches in her own terms, but she can do so only after his death. Moreover, the heyday of the porch, which ended in the late 1960s, occurred before women largely transitioned from inside to outside the home for work. The porch, during this era, was not only a site of struggle for mothers and children. It also was a place for men, women, and children to vie for control. In the following stories, we will see how the porch brought men into the domestic world of the family, but we will also see how the public, patriarchal authority of men has, at times, granted them a certain degree of porch privilege.

A MAN'S "SPACE"

Many informants have communicated to me that the men in their family typically have used the porch for socializing and relaxation, a place to rest after they get home from work and on weekends. Remember, from the first chapter, how my father's father used the porch as a place for Bible study and to help the African American preacher prepare his text for the next day. My grandfather was certainly gendering the space as "male," where two men engaged in biblical study. But is he not also gendering the space as "female" when he is engaged in the rearing of his children? Already we have an example of how the gendering of the porch is not necessarily tidy.

We have been looking at stories in which children use porches to seize limited power. The following account by Sharra Kirvin, a former student of mine, renders a family narrative set in Appalachicola, Florida, circa 1961, when one "bad boy" used his porch to literally keep ties with his grandfather:

> My dad was more of a troublemaker as a young child than anyone I know or ever will know, for that matter. . . . My dad always enjoyed his grandfather's visits. He enjoyed getting to see him so much that often he would do just about anything to keep him from leaving. When begging, crying, and stalling wouldn't make him stay, he took matters into his own hands. He found a big rope and tied my great-grandfather's truck to the columns of the porch. Since he was rather unobservant, my great-grandfather never even noticed the rope. When he drove off, he took the porch with him and didn't even realize it until he was halfway to town.

Men weren't always the victims of children's pranks, though. The following account, provided by Joyce Hebert Babin as she remembers her grandfather, Felix J. Lambert, shows how men could embrace the everyday, familial pleasures of the porch, particularly in their storytelling events:

> My grandparents lived next door to us when I was growing up in the thirties. Each night after Grandpa ate his supper, we three sisters watched from our house to see him come out on his porch, recline in his rocker, and prop up his feet on the post. This was our cue to run over there, sit on the edge of the porch to listen to his delightful stories. Some were pure fiction—right out of his head. Others were "true stories" from his lifetime. He usually told us if they were true, but sometimes he just enjoyed letting us guess—"Pa, did that really happen?"—And he would give us one of those "What do you think?" toothless grins.
>
> His reason for starting this ritual, besides simply loving to tell stories, was to keep us from going to movies too often. "They're bad for your eyes," he'd say. After he learned that we enjoyed the Saturday night serials at the theatre,

which were continued from week to week, he started telling us stories "to be continued," leaving us in suspense all week (which gave him time to think of an ending).

Our very favorite was the saga of "Jacques and Saraphine," a married Cajun couple living through hard times (most of Pa's stories were told to us in French). Saraphine was a very pious woman. Jacques, on the other hand, was rather mischievous and kept getting into trouble. His loving wife went to great extremes to bail him out and to try to reform him. Pa would often have us rolling on the porch in laughter—especially with his sound effects.

Grandma would come out after a while and sit in her rocker with her fan. When it started getting dark and Ma's fan was slapping mosquitoes too frequently, we knew it was time to go home and dream about the adventures we had experienced on Ma and Pa's front porch.

This is not just a grandmother's porch, a phrase we have encountered frequently in our stories; it is, rather, "Ma and Pa's front porch." And "Pa" seems every bit as engaged in rearing his grandchildren so that they will lead "a virtuous life" as the mothers in earlier accounts did. The porch here is, again, a "device of social control," portraying men as actively engaged in the life of the children.

Robert R. Thomas, of Swansboro, North Carolina, recalls sharing the porch with his grandfather:

After [Sunday] dinner (in the South, "dinner" is after church, "supper" is in the evening, and there ain't no "lunch"!), everyone would retreat to their various nooks and crannies to unfasten their belts and doze awhile. My Paw Paw would head for the front porch. He pulled his chair up close to the brick column, so he could prop up his feet, dug in his pocket for his Barlow knife and began to sharpen it. He'd apply a little spit to the stone and slowly and patiently slide the blade around in a circle on the stone. He'd sharpen each blade until he could shave the hair from his arm. Then he would pick up the Sunday paper and begin to read. As he finished each section, he would re-fold it and drop it on the floor beside him. I always watched and waited for the "funnies," or comics, to drop, and I would grab them and devour that week's stories about Dick Tracy, Lil' Abner, Nancy and Sluggo, Joe Palooka and others.

As I was reading, Paw Paw would step to the edge of the porch and cut a limb from a shrub. Then he would sit down, prop up his feet and begin to whittle. First, he stripped the bark in long strings and let them fall to the floor. Then he would trim up the ends of the twig and make sure they were smooth. Then he might cut a few rings around the twig, or whittle away one end or the other. Sometimes he just whittled until it was gone. Other times he would make "something" and give it to me. When he was finished, he would kick the shavings into the yard and hand me the stick while turning to go inside. Usually, he thrust the stick at me with a grunted "H'Ya' Go," and walk into the house. (1–2)

While not engaged in the traditional activities of storytelling, gossip, and conversation, this Paw Paw is certainly engaged in establishing a relationship with his grandson, by whittling "things" for him on the porch.

Marsha Wells, who grew up in New Orleans, also remembers sharing a front porch with her maternal grandfather. Her grandmother passed away before Marsha was born, so her memories are with her grandfather. Marsha said that her "mother used to go by my grandfather's almost every weekend, and sometimes during the week." She remembers sharing evenings with her grandfather "to cool off." The family had window fans, and would sit outside until it "cooled off well enough to go in the house." When she and her grandfather shared the porch swing, he would tell the young Marsha "all kinds of stories about when he was a little boy, about country life." Marsha's grandfather, who grew up in rural Pointe Coupee Parish, wished to communicate to his first grandchild, the only girl, his family history.

Michael Cavanaugh, who has given us several stories so far, shared the following thoughts to challenge the gendering of the porch as strictly female:

I don't ever remember seeing any women on the porch except just in transition. But now I gathered it was by their choice. They were always laughing— there were seven women, four men—they were always back in the kitchen, the dining room. Now as for politics, my grandfather was a politician—he was a legislator, a sheriff, and he was tax assessor for thirty-five years—and he was a Long ally. My aunt told me she actually saw Huey Long on the front porch delivering materials and talking to the men. I was trying to get proof that he spent the night there, but I never could. It was a political place, that's true. The men, they would be talking politics, always. We were a political family. I don't think of the porch as a feminine place.

Marsha M. Wells with her grandfather, Marshall Eli Colar, New Orleans, La., ca. 1956.
(Photograph courtesy of Marsha M. Wells)

Michael Cavanaugh is talking here about his "grandmother's" porch. In theory, his grandmother controls this place. In reality, she is working in the kitchen while the men talk politics on the porch. Michael Cavanaugh's experiences of this 1960s porch as a man's space could be because he visited his grandmother during family gatherings. And women, who were in charge of preparing the food, rarely found the time to talk politics on the porch. But Cavanaugh sees some element of choice in the division of space; the women certainly had their share of fun in the kitchen, while the men reminisced about the politics of Huey Long. The public nature of the porch fell prey to the public world of politics, so at these times it was defined less by the dynamics of the home and domesticity and more by the demands of the larger political system, a system that during this era consigned women to the kitchen and (white) men to Congress.

The porch in Cavanaugh's story is, despite all of the political dynamics, primarily a *social* space where the men spend holidays swapping political *gossip*. Indeed, while women might traditionally frame the porch in storytelling and gossip, it is often more because of opportunity than natural inclination. Mattie Lou (Faroldo) Furby, who grew up in Colfax, Louisiana, remembers her father, "Mr. Clarence," as a porch storyteller. She says, "He entertained us all with his stories. Whether they were true or not, it didn't matter. They provided everyone with laughs and left us with fond memories to carry to our grandchildren."

Storytelling and gossip among men also frame William Faulkner's *Absalom, Absalom!* In this novel, the narrative structure of which is driven by oral storytelling, Faulkner shows how the men of Jefferson, Mississippi, become ensnared in porch gossip aimed at resolving the enigmatic details of Thomas Sutpen's life. We have already talked about how the young, "white trash" Thomas Sutpen started the "whole story" by being spurned by a slave from a "rich plantation owner's" portico. Sutpen's story lives on to entrap the future citizens of Jefferson, even those who live one hundred years after him. His story has particularly gripped members of the Compson family, who have spent much of their lives on their front porch listening to their father's wild, erroneous speculations about Sutpen's life story. Near the beginning of the novel, Quentin Compson and his father have come together on the porch swing after supper — at twilight, itself a transitional period between daylight and dark. In this transitional state at this transitional site, Quentin listens to his father's overpowering, wildly speculative gossip about the Sutpens. On his father's decaying gallery, symbolic of the decaying plantation culture, Quentin meets the ghosts of his past. He listens — though not hungrily — to his father's gossip, which is his grandfather's gossip, which is Sutpen's, which is the town's. The gossip in Faulkner's novel is not a benign form of social control, however. It is an overpowering obsession that ultimately contributes to Quentin's self-destruction. Or to use the words of Judith Sutpen, words delivered through Mr. Compson:

You get born and you try this and you dont know why only you keep on trying it and you are born at the same time with a lot of other people, all mixed up with them, like trying to, having to, move your arms and legs with strings only the same strings are hitched to all the other arms and legs and the others all trying and they dont know why either except that the strings are all in one another's way like five or six people all trying to make a rug on the same loom only each one wants to weave his own pattern into the rug. (157)

Individual characters in *Absalom, Absalom!* indeed attempt to weave their own pattern into this "rug on the same loom," venturing to own it. But the tyrannical plantation narrative of Thomas Sutpen has become so inextricably woven into the community's fabric of gossip that any "authentic" version of Sutpen's story is, for all intents and purposes, unrecoverable. Sutpen's public authority and power have overpowered the citizens of Jefferson.

Because the porch incorporates the male world of public authority and power, it can also function as a site for economic transactions. Emma Major echoes the porch as more of a semipublic institution for men, calling it a "poor man's office where workers were paid their wages, and hiring and firing took place." Of course, Major's observation assumes that the porch owner maintains employees to hire and fire. Hers is not the perspective of, say, a sharecropper, or of the young Thomas Sutpen in Faulkner's *Absalom, Absalom!* Although the porch can be a "poor man's" office, it is, nonetheless, just that—an *office*, indicating some sort of economic power that can be displayed publicly.

Indeed, Emma Major's designation of the porch in terms of economics makes us wonder what the space means for men who have not conformed to traditional notions of patriarchy. The following story, whose teller I leave unnamed because of the story's intensely personal nature, is a poignant representation of how the porch functioned for a man who, for a time, did not altogether meet with society's expectations:

Our front porch was used mostly by my father. He loved that front porch. When he and my mother married, his grandfather had started this lumber company at home, and it was a big business, you know. He had it made. And they opened one in [another town]. His uncle was in charge of it. He had a very bright future. And then the Depression came, and the lumber company gradually folded up. So he was without work for a long time. Then he built a kiln. He did that for a while, and it didn't do well. And he closed that down, and then he built a retail lumber yard, and did that for a while. And it didn't do very well. . . . Whereas mother . . . my mother was the hardest working.

Shaping the Family

That's why this picture—this is very personal—but this picture of my daddy with his feet propped up on the banister sitting on the porch while mother was inside cooking dinner, cleaning up, and then going and practicing for church, to play, in her spare time. And finally, she's the one—she was a wonderful cook—and the restaurant on Main Street was up for sale, so she decided . . . She talked him into their buying the restaurant. And that's what put us all through school, that restaurant business. Both worked very hard there. (Unnamed, July 12, 1996)

During our interview, this storyteller's delivery was halting—and quite moving. She even gripped her chest while talking. When I first heard this story, I assumed that the teller was confronting some of the resentment she felt at her father's openly displaying to the community his momentary lack of enterprise. But I had made the error of imposing a 1990s sensibility on a 1930s story. Earlier, we read Doreen Massey's statement that "spaces and places . . . are gendered in a myriad different ways, which vary between cultures and over time." Had the story been told today, or even before the Depression, my first response would perhaps have been more on target. But this is a 1930s Depression story, when men who were displaced often found themselves at home and were, nevertheless, not required to help in domestic affairs because of the strict codification of gender roles. But such established roles were not without resentment.

The teller of the above story corrected my first impression, telling me that her resentment was not because of his economic hardships, which were not uncommon in the 1930s. Rather, she resented her father's not doing more to help her mother in her chores. But, as the teller says, "That was a different era, and I understand that" (e-mail corresp., July 16, 1999). The teller's mother had little time for the porch, and when she did sit on the porch, she "was always working . . . snapping beans and such." Because of the mother's willingness to be "the hardest working," her children were able to go to college. Is this a porch that feels the public authority of patriarchal power? If it is a man's "place," it is certainly not one of power in the conventional sense. While the father does seem to bear the privilege of resting his feet on the porch, the family's economic success stems from the mother, who toils inside the home. Such a story should make us reluctant, when discussing the porch as a "male space," to do so in uncomplicated terms of male dominance.

Moreover, men have used the porch in simple, everyday, even domestic ways. We have already heard about men whittling, gossiping, and storytelling. Nell Coleman tells the following story of her father, who had a country house in Brookhaven, Mississippi:

> At one point in time we had a well where you'd have to draw water, before my parents got a water line out there. And then after the well, they had gotten running water, but you had to have a pump to run water in the house. But I can remember when we'd have to draw water from the well. And . . . especially Daddy . . . he liked this big old wooden bucket. And he'd have a thing that was hanging down, and he'd hang his bucket on that. Anyway, he'd like to have his little wash pan and his towel and his water bucket with a dipper in it. And he'd dip out some water and put it in his little wash basin and wash his hands out on the front porch. Right in front of the porch, we had calla lilies, and we'd dump the water out there, and that would water the plants, and they'd grow like crazy.

Mrs. Coleman's father had a strong relationship with his porch. In fact, when I asked Mrs. Coleman who got more use of the front porch, her mother or her father, she said: "I think probably Daddy did because he had a little bit more spare time. Mama was always . . . she had the field and she always cooked and she had six kids. Daddy couldn't boil water." One is tempted to invoke the old proverb here: A man works from sun to sun, but a woman's work is never done. In spite of the fact that Mrs. Coleman's mother was at home all day while her father's primary work was away from the house, the father was still perceived to get more use of the front porch "because he had a little bit more spare time."

To be fair, though, men, particularly in the days of the agrarian South, have done their share of toil on the porch. Leon Deshotels, an eighty-something Cajun man from Mansura, Louisiana, tells the following story of when he was growing up during the 1930s:

> We made our own rice. Every year we'd plant so much. That was a slough back there, belonged to my grandfather. We called that a "coulee." When it was almost ready to cut, you'd take your plant just like potatoes. And we had to go in the water and just stick 'em in there with our finger. It wasn't deep. So we'd cut that rice and put it to dry on the porch or upstairs. Then when the

cool weather came up, we'd make what we call a "coup de main," a helping hand. The farmers would come. And they had a big, wide board that had some big holes. And two or three men would get on each side, and when one would knock, the other would spool it, you see, up after he hit the sticks. And I had an old l'oncle—uncle—he was always saying things and he was running the thing. He was hollering. Oh, you could hear that for a mile, when they were beating the rice as it went through from the shell. That rice would go through those little holes. And if there was enough, we'd haul it upstairs. And whenever we wanted some rice, we'd go upstairs and get some.

The sense of a community of farmers, a community of men, is strikingly clear here, as the men come together to lend a "coup de main," a helping hand. To the sounds of his "l'oncle," Deshotels's family went through the winnowing procedure to produce its supply of rice, which was stored upstairs.

And though none of my informants have spoken of other male work activities, we can imagine that there certainly must have been many in the various regions of the South. The rural, yeoman farmer certainly used his porch to store machinery and tools. The kind of machinery or tool would depend on the work done in the region, of course. The photographs here illustrate the work associated with tobacco curing in Georgia and muskrat trapping in Louisiana. Other families would see their porches function as workshops for the repair of small motors or large appliances, or even the construction of projects or repairing of furniture. Woodworking could certainly go beyond whittling. The porch has indeed been able to bring together communities of men to get the necessary work done, whatever that work might be, while sometimes seizing a bit of pleasure.

FAMILIES THAT FUNCTION

Most of the stories we have read in this chapter illustrate how mothers, fathers, children, neighbors, and friends come together to create a sense of family and community. They are similar to Mattie Lou (Faroldo) Furby's account of a typical Sunday afternoon on the front porch:

On Saturday afternoon, my parents would bake a pound cake or a jelly cake (made with fresh mayhaw jelly) to be served to family and friends who dropped by on Sunday afternoon. Cake and coffee was served on the front porch. Sometimes the ladies would sit on the porch while the men gathered in the living

Sharecroppers grade cured tobacco leaves on the porch and sort them for the tobacco auction near Douglas, Ga. (Photograph by Dorothea Lange, 1938; Library of Congress, Prints and Photographs Division [LC-USF34-018710-E])

Men grading muskrats while fur buyers and Spanish trappers look on during an auction sale on the porch of a community store in St. Bernard, Louisiana. (Photograph by Marion Post Wolcott, 1941; Library of Congress, Prints and Photographs Division [LC-USF33-031173-M3])

room to watch a ballgame on television. The local Catholic priest would often join us. One of our cousins who lived in Shreveport would call to say she would come for a visit on Sunday, so "please save me a place on the front porch."

As this story indicates, the porch works when a family and community members share power on the porch, when women, men, and even children can use the "space" to exercise some part of their individual identity.

Dorothy M. Alford, the daughter of a Methodist minister, details the daily uses of her family's different porches. Alford, now of Crystal Springs, Mississippi, was "reared in a dozen or so" Mississippi towns as her father went from church to church. Despite the family's migratory patterns, though, "the porch," taken in its totality, has come to "symbolize security" for Dorothy Alford because of her family's continued uses during a "typical day in [their] parsonage":

To begin the day, the porch was by far the most pleasant work-place we had. To my sister, just older than I, and to me fell the tasks of stringing beans and shelling peas and butterbeans from our father's garden in order that our table at noon would be loaded for a family of seven. We loved being on the porch for we could watch our dog outside and talk with him; there were always interesting neighbors whose comings and goings we could later report to Mama; the hydrant in the yard gave us excuses for many trips for a drink when our fingertips became sore from recalcitrant immature beans. Best of all, we could dress in our coolest clothes and shun footwear of any kind.

Afternoons were quite different! The porch was swept and ready for entertainment. Mama and her lady friends, fresh and tidy after the morning's work, had the porch as their undisputed domain. Conversation, uninterrupted by radio or television, was the order of the day. Sometimes there was cake to be shared, or, wonder of wonders, Mama's refreshing "Blackberry Acid" to be sipped.

As the day progressed and the friends went home "to see about supper," our family gathered on the porch, reluctant to give it up during the last moments of light. But it is my night memories of our porches that I enjoy most. Because I was the baby, my bedtime came early; the other children had school work or other activities; Mama and Daddy sat on the porch. During their quiet time together, they discussed the joys and problems of the congregation. Today I can still feel the coolness of the sheets of my bed near the open window and can hear the soft, low tones of my father's voice and the murmur of my mother's replies. I can see the occasional glow of Daddy's pipe and the staccato trail of a lightning bug as I drifted into sleep. It is no wonder that our porches of old have come to symbolize security to me.

Alford's caring detail portrays a "day in the life of a porch" — one that belongs to an entire family—as gender and generational roles are defined and negotiated. The porch begins as the daughters' space for work and play in the morning. The two sisters are tasked with "stringing beans" and "shelling peas," but they occasionally break free from their chores to take trips to the water hydrant. Thus, they find their ways of defining a sense of pleasure in their assigned work. In the afternoons, the porch becomes the mother's "undisputed domain" as she gathers with her "lady friends" to share conversation (or gossip). At night, the parents finally have a space for their "quiet time together." The young Dorothy overhears the "low tones of [her] father's voice and the murmur of [her] mother's replies." At night, when the parents come together to "discuss the joys and problems of the congregation," the father takes control of the conversation (or perhaps even gossip), while the mother softly replies. The young Dorothy falls asleep in the security of a traditional southern family. And in this functioning family, there seems to be respect for the traditional roles that have been assigned to the women, the men, and the children. Ultimately, the porch is not a "woman's space" or a "man's space" or a "child's space" or a "community space." It is a "liminal space" where all of these roles are negotiated within families and communities.

Alford tells a porch story that most of us want to remember, and some of us can: the security of a community, the preparation of available and good food, the warmth of loving parents. The young Dorothy's position as eavesdropper to her parents' nighttime murmurs perhaps best represents her safe and protected world. The parents here, while seeking their much-desired privacy, nevertheless keep watch on the porch, ready to shield the family of seven from outside harm.

Not all children are so lucky, however. June Chachere Carriere, who lives with her husband of fifty-eight years, has poignant stories of her father as he lay dying on the family's front porch when Carriere was only eighteen months old. The family home, located in Opelousas, Louisiana, was built in 1826 and was bought by June Carriere's mother in 1921, after the father passed away. Carriere and her husband returned to the family home after World War II and have lived there ever since, making restorations as they are needed. Today, she and her family sit on the porch where the father lay dying over seventy years ago. Carriere has two memories of her father: One is of his lying on a cot on the porch, which was "screened-in in those days" (she has since rebuilt the porch). She remembers approaching her father as a tiny girl, wearing one of his neckties—something he apparently didn't like. Her first and only memory of her father is of his fussing at her from his cot for wearing his necktie.

Her second memory is of her mother singing the following song to her father, as he lay dying:

> Sing me to sleep, the shadows fall,
> Let me forget the world and all.
> Sad is my heart, the day is long,
> Come let me hear the evening song.
> Sing me to sleep and let me rest,
> In all the world, I love you best.
> Nothing is faithful, nothing is true
> In heaven and earth but God and you.
> Love, I am lonely; days are so long,
> I want you only, you and your song.
> Dark is life's story, night is so deep,
> Leave me no more, dear, sing me to sleep.

Carriere, in our interview, sang this stirring song for me, recalling her mother's singing to the dying father. The song evoked a range of emotions: the security of a mother's singing, juxtaposed with the memory of a father dying. There is no abuse in this story—only the sense of loss.

As a tangible reminder of her father's existence, a wisteria bush grows on the edge of June Carriere's porch—one that he saw planted at his request before he died. When her children move into new homes, they each will come to the family place to pick and plant a piece of their grandfather's wisteria bush. Doing so serves as a touching reminder that his presence in the family has been more spiritual than physical.

While June Carriere grew up without two parents, she nevertheless grew up in a loving home with the sense of security. But this is not always the case. If this

Home of June C. and John Allie Carriere, Opelousas, La.
(Photograph by Jon Griffin Donlon, 1999)

study is to be fair, it should give voice to those children who did not drift off to sleep between cool, crisp sheets, feeling safe in a protected world.

"BORN ON THE WRONG SIDE OF THE PORCH"

Obviously, not every family with a porch is necessarily functional. As Doreen Massey says, "The home may be as much a place of conflict . . . as of repose. . . . Many women have had to *leave* home precisely in order to forge their own version of their identity" (11).

Family stories told to me by Jane McManus Schoen and her sister, Susan McManus, illustrate themes of leaving home. These two sisters contacted me for

June Carriere (on swing), her husband, John Allie, and her sister Lillian C. Mayne (sewing). (Photograph by Jon Griffin Donlon, 1999)

an interview because they had put together a family cookbook, to be given out at the McManus family reunion at the homeplace in Meadville, in 1994. They titled their cookbook *The Front Porch* and included an illustration of the family porch on the cover. The front porch symbolized for the two sisters the coming together of their extended family. Indeed, their cousin, Phil Aurit Jr., in the foreword to the cookbook, talks of his own feelings about the family porch:

> After thinking about my recollections of Mississippi, I came to realize that there was a particular place on the old farm where important events took place. It wasn't where I would have expected it to be, the living room. Or as

Shaping the Family

McManus family porch, Meadville, Miss. (Photograph courtesy of Jane Schoen)

essential as the preparation and consumption of good food was, it wasn't even the kitchen. The significant place was where, as a boy from Los Angeles 37 years ago, I shot a rifle for the first time. And where this past June, I saw my mother sit and rock contentedly for hour upon hour. It is also the place where all the McManus families and the entire McManus family gathered for pictures at the family reunion. It was also the place from where I was struck by what a large organic unit the clan really was. Yes, the front porch of the old farm house played a big part in our past and the reunion.

It did my heart good to watch my mother up on that porch rock away and look quite happy to be there. She didn't talk to me much when I was a boy about her life on the farm. It was my impression that she was glad to leave Mississippi and move to the West Coast. She was ready to take the jump, along with my father, to leave farm life behind and start a new, more citified life far away. There was promise of reward elsewhere and she was determined to make a go of it wherever "it" might lead.

Shaping the Family

In talking of their grandparents' porch in Meadville, Mississippi, members of the McManus family inevitably talk about leaving home—particularly the women in the family. Phil's mother left for California, in search of a new life. The family was poor, with eight children, so the motivation to escape was likely the search for additional space and privacy. Jane and Susan had a difficult time, when putting together their cookbook that was accompanied by pictures and family stories, actually getting many memories from the living members of the immediate family. They were attempting to erase the difficulty of a life of poverty in a poor section of the South. Susan told me, "When Phil's mother went to California, it was over. She didn't want anybody to know about her past." Phil's mother's sibling, "Aunt Vel," left home, married an Englishman, was abandoned by him, and eventually returned to the homeplace to commit suicide in her late sixties. When I told Jane and Susan that I would love to know Aunt Vel's relationship to the front porch, they speculated that "she probably saw it as an anchor." All of the McManus men went on to become millionaires; the women went on to live somewhat unhappy lives. The McManus father was "horribly strict," according to Jane and Susan. A family friend even told Jane and Susan that the only way their aunts could have any interaction with young men was "to flirt with their brothers' friends." Small wonder they wanted to escape the family home in Meadville. Given such oppressive circumstances, the thoughts of Phil's mother on that front porch were likely very conflicted. In this nostalgic image, we get the picture of a woman who, at best, comes to find some kind of peace while wrestling with a troubled background.

The McManus family reminds us that our nostalgia about home and porch must be tempered with a realistic view of troubled families. Another such reminder comes from the contemporary novelist, poet, and essayist Dorothy Allison. In her autobiographical essays, Allison talks in painfully frank terms of having to leave her home in order to escape her stepfather's sexual and physical abuse, to escape poverty, to escape a culture in which women found themselves pregnant at fourteen, as did her own mother.

Allison's semiautobiographical novel, *Bastard Out of Carolina*, takes us into the private, terrifying world of Ruth Anne Boatwright, nicknamed "Bone," a young, poverty-stricken little girl who suffers physical and sexual abuse at the hands of her stepfather, Daddy Glen Waddell. To tell Bone's devastating story of abuse,

Shaping the Family

Allison uses the front porch to reveal how Bone's family operates outside of established traditions and norms. As we saw in the previous chapter, Bone was "born on the wrong side of the porch" (54); she is not a product of middle-class courtship traditions that are sanctioned by our culture, traditions that eventually lead to a stable marriage and family; rather, according to others, she is "illegitimate white trash." And while Bone does exploit the liminality of the porch, using its public side to limit heterosexual encounters, her motives stem from perversions of sexuality: the semipublic safety of her grandmother's front porch enables Bone to escape her stepfather's abuse.

When we first meet Bone, we discover that she has been "certified a bastard by the state of South Carolina" (3). The courthouse stamp seals her identity as "illegitimate white trash." Because Bone's parents never married, she has grown up without the legacy of mythologizing courtship stories. Elizabeth Stone has observed in her book, Black Sheep and Kissing Cousins: "The courtship story tends to be a staple in any family which tells stories at all. This is because the courtship story bears the same relation to the new family as a creation myth does to any larger culture or civilization. The courtship story is the story of How the Family Began, or this branch at any rate. It is the first collective memory of the new family, paradoxically shared even by children who were unborn at the time" (64). The origins of Bone's family, however, are not mythologized. Her father is a villain; no one talks about him except to "curse his name" (26). So Bone has no authenticating courtship-creation myth, one for which she truly longs. She says, "It wasn't even that I was so insistent on knowing anything about my missing father. I wouldn't have minded a lie. I just wanted the story Mama would have told" (31). Bone simply wants the creation myth.

Anney Boatwright, Bone's mother, does try to create a "mythical" nuclear family with her second husband, Glen Waddell. Glen is the son of a local white patriarch who seems hell-bent on alienating his wealthy family by marrying "white trash." And in his attempts to court Anney, Glen uses her mother's porch to cross over into a different class. He would "come over, meet her girls, sit on her porch and talk a little" (15). Daddy Glen even tries to seal his bond with Anney by taking "family pictures" on the porch.

However, Glen and Anney's pictures reveal the dysfunction in this emerging relationship. Bone describes the photo shoot in these terms:

From the other side of Earle's truck, I stood and looked back at them, Granny up on the porch with her hesitant uncertain smile, and Mama down on the steps in her new blouse with Glen in that short brush haircut, while Alma posed on the walkway focusing up at them. Everybody looked nervous but determined, Mama stiff in Glen's awkward embrace and Glen almost stumbling off the steps as he tried to turn his face away from the camera. It made my neck go tight just to look at them. (39)

Porch pictures are traditionally celebratory occasions during which crowds of folks gather in a semipublic setting to record their shared identity. However, for Bone these family pictures with Daddy Glen are malevolent. Because the posing family members are on public exhibition, they attempt to fall into traditional behaviors—smiling, arranging themselves strategically on the porch, walkways, and steps. But because Glen cannot look fully into the camera, these photographs warn of the private domestic terrors yet to come, making Bone's "neck go tight just to look at them."

These sinister porch photographs threaten what is a relatively secure world for Bone. When living at their grandmother's house, Bone, her little sister Reese, and their mother Anney have a safe life, particularly on the porch of the Boatwright home. However, their porch life is not romanticized in traditional terms. Indeed, in describing one summer evening, Bone portrays the life of her grandmother's "white trash" porch in terms of anti-romance:

> I edged forward until I could put my hand on Granny's chair. . . . The laughter echoed around me. . . . Granny put her arm down and squeezed my wrist. She leaned over and spat a stream of brown snuff off the side of the porch. I heard the dull plopping sound it made as it landed in the dusty yard. I slipped under her shoulder, leaned across the side of the rocker, and put my face close to her breast. I could smell wet snap beans, tobacco, lemon juice on her neck, and a little sharp piss scent, and a little salt. . . . I laughed up into her neck. . . . I rocked myself against her, as happy and safe as Little Earle had felt with her teeth on his belly. (20–21)

Bone is "happy and safe" on her grandmother's porch, but in her images of spitting tobacco, piss scents, and salt smells, she doesn't let us forget that we are about as far away from the mythologized nuclear family as we can get. This is the porch of a poor Carolina family. Most of the daughters are pregnant by the age of fifteen. Bone's grandmother even says, when comforting Bone about her court-house stamp of "bastard": "Did [people] ask to see your birth certificate before they sat themselves on your porch?" (3). The porch for Granny is a place where pretensions are nonexistent. Although situated in poverty and illegitimacy, the Boatwright family porch is nevertheless a celebrated place for telling stories, drinking iced tea, potting flowers, and playing children's games. It is a place to which Bone returns for comfort once Anney and Daddy Glen get married. Indeed, it is a place to which Bone returns for safety, where she can temporarily escape the terrors that lie beyond the threshold of her own home.

Such permanence and safety on her grandmother's porch stand in stark con-trast to the emptiness of Daddy Glen's houses. In fact, Bone's grandmother "always complained about [Anney] not living in houses with porches and rock-ing chairs" (143). Bone lives in a series of "rented houses; houses leased with an option to buy; shared houses on the city limits; brick and stucco and a prom-ise to buy" (64). In the words of Temple, Bone's cousin, Daddy Glen always rented "unloved" houses for his family—houses that looked "naked and aban-doned," houses where "it look[ed] like nobody every really wanted to live" (79). Daddy Glen imagines that these porchless, barren tract houses proclaim a higher status, separating his family from the Boatwrights' working-class fare of "big old rickety houses with wide porches and dogs lying out flat in the sun" (79).

When Bone enters Daddy Glen's unloved homes, she crosses the threshold into terror, where she is victim of physical abuse so violent that it repeatedly lands her in emergency rooms with broken bones, and where she must endure the ter-rifying sexual violations of Daddy Glen, who holds his body "tight to [Bone's], his hands shaking as they moved restlessly, endlessly, over [her] belly, ass, and thighs" (108). The parent, in Bone's case, is not the sentry who stands ready to protect her from defilement; rather he is the transgressor who violently defiles, who sends her running to her grandmother's and to her aunts' porches for safety.

Bone's violent history of the porch is inextricably tied up with class bound-aries, where she is judged as "born on the wrong side of the porch" because she is poor, white, and illegitimate. For a young girl of the 1950s, before the law offered much protection for girls—particularly poor girls—who were victims of domes-tic abuse, escaping to even the "wrong side" of a "rickety" porch was better than crossing the threshold to where horrors awaited within. Bone's history of the porch is, in addition, tied to her notions of sexuality, albeit perversions of hetero-sexuality. It is difficult to imagine the young girl surviving such domestic abuse. And yet she does manage to position herself as a survivor. As we will see in the next chapter, which focuses on courtship, romance, and sexuality, Bone is able to use the "rickety" porches of her life for personal, even sexual, power.

5: FANNING THE FLAMES

Because the porch is a liminal space somewhere between public and private, it is, as we have seen, subject to the pressures of the community without, as well as to the authority of the household within. Few porch activities demonstrate the pressures of this liminality better than those associated with courtship, romance, and sexuality. Indeed, tradition tells us that the porch is a safe, semipublic site for heterosexual romance rituals: It is private enough for the whispering of sweet nothings between a young man and woman, but it is also public enough for parents to imagine that the family name will not be threatened by inappropriate displays of sexual activity.

Such established traditions of porch romance typically celebrate the nuclear, middle- to upper-class family, headed by both a mother and father who have had several to many children. And I do not want to discount these stories. But, from this traditional context, I turn to courtship stories from the Other side of the porch in order to include stories told by gays and lesbians as well as by heterosexuals. How does the porch figure in their lives? Is it a "space" or a "place"? In the previous chapter, we looked at how Dorothy Allison depicts the darker side of the porch in her novel *Bastard Out of Carolina*. Her main character, Bone, says that she was "born on the wrong side of the porch" (54); the young girl is not a product of middle-class traditions and norms; rather, she is considered "illegitimate white trash" who, as we have already heard, comes from the "wrong side" of the porch. Moreover, Bone is just beginning to become aware of her lesbianism, so her alienation from traditional, heterosexual courtship rituals is even further intensified.

As Allison shows, courtship is inevitably tied to class as well as to sexual orientation. Traditional, middle-class notions of porch courtship certainly rest on presumptions of heterosexuality, as the following stories will illustrate.

To establish traditional, heterosexual notions of Southern porch romance, I will start with my own lower-middle-class, white, nuclear family. My family owes its origin to my parents' front-porch romance, which began in 1945 in Lake Charles, Louisiana, at the home of my maternal grandparents, Richard and Florence Foreman. Indeed, thirty-two years later, when my grandmother passed away, my father, Calvin Hazelwood, took my grandparents' porch swing home with him to guard his memories of having courted my mother on it under the watchful eye of my grandparents, particularly my grandmother. My grandmother was so strict that she even refused to let my mother go to Opelousas, my father's hometown, to choose her own wedding ring. My dad's sister, Vera, selected it for her (and I am wearing it today).

My favorite family story of porch romance, told to me by my mother, Marie Hazelwood, was that on the evening in 1946 when my parents decided to marry, the young couple saw a falling star while sitting on my grandparents' porch swing, which they bought when they got married. My father, a twenty-six-year-old Southern Baptist minister, wondered aloud to my mother if the end of the world was coming to take the romantic couple into paradise (and he was not joking). The porch was not only a transitional space between public and private spheres for this pair; it was a possible passage from this earth to the New Jerusalem. This porch story, for me, reveals my parents' belief in their destiny to be together on earth *and* in paradise—a belief that comforted my mother for the sixteen years that she lived as a widow, and a belief that somehow comforts me now that they both have passed away.

Other family stories that I have collected also bear out meaningful traditions of porch courtship and romance in the South. For example, Leon Deshotels from Mansura, Louisiana (the same Mr. Deshotels who described the winnowing of rice in the previous chapter), spoke to me of courting his first girlfriend on her parents' front porch during the Great Depression:

> My first girlfriend, her name was Adele de Glandon. Beautiful girl. And I'd walk that six miles to go to her house. . . . I was seeing Adele, and her sister also had a boyfriend. And I was at this end, and he was at the other end. And the old lady [Adele's mother] was sitting in the middle of the house—just in-

Florence and Richard Foreman on the family "courting" swing, Lake Charles, La.,
ca. 1960. (Photograph in author's possession)

side the house. You wouldn't see her. . . . Oh yeah, you wouldn't see her. But
she was there—within shotgun reach!

From her private watch, Adele de Glandon's mother fully intended to protect the
public reputation of her daughters from such rascals as Leon Deshotels. She sat
between the courting couples, right inside the house, right within shotgun reach,
buttressed by her authority that extended from within the home, safeguarding
the family reputation that lay beyond the threshold—even if it meant resorting
to the shotgun.

When the time came for Deshotels to court Nester Roy, the woman he was to
marry in the 1930s, he tried to gain some distance from the watchful eye of his
future mother-in-law—and to get closer to his girlfriend—by courting on the
back porch swing: "Well, I'd walk about five miles to see [Nester]. And we'd sit

out on the back porch, not on the front porch. The swing was on the back porch. They had a front porch, but there was a swing on the back porch, so we could sit close." Dodging the shotgun and gaining the swing, where the two could "sit close," Deshotels, who is still quite the charmer in his mid-eighties, won the heart of Nester Roy. His story speaks to a time when the South was more agrarian than industrial, when men walked five to six miles to court women on their own space.

During this era of home courtship, part of the porch courting game was to find a moment of privacy in an intensely public space. Michael Cavanaugh offers an amusing example of how young lovers can make creative use of the "space" of the porch to gain privacy. When I asked if he remembered any courtship stories from his family home in DeRidder, Louisiana, he responded:

> The only one I remember was told to me by my Aunt Azalee. (Azalea is actually her name. The family corrupted it to Azalee, but she still prefers Azalea.) She told me that she and my uncle A.J.—there used to be a side porch around on the side that doesn't now have a porch; there used to be a little freestanding lean-to porch—she and Uncle A.J. would climb on top of that porch and sit on the roof to do their courting because it was the only place they could have any privacy. Now when this house was originally built, there was a room right at the end of the porch that had no doors anywhere except on the porch; it was an entertainment room. Subsequently, in my grandmother's old age, they made a door connected to the rest of the house, but when that house was designed and built, that room was off the porch, and it was supposedly the one place for privacy. But Aunt Azalee said they didn't get it, so they climbed on top of the porch.

Clearly, the Cavanaugh front porch was more public than private for these teenagers; there was no secluded back porch with a swing, as there was for the young Leon and Nester. So the couple was compelled to circumvent the public nature of the porch by climbing onto its roof, exploiting their youthful agility. Also noteworthy is how the "privacy room," which one could enter only from the porch, was off limits for the young Azalee, perhaps because it was *too* private—not liminal enough—and therefore inappropriate. Azalee and her suitor were thus forced to seek more desperate measures, turning their energy to creative uses of the porch roof.

Fanning the Flames

Sometimes gaining such privacy was not so difficult. Myra Pellowski, who grew up in Baton Rouge, tells of the porch's being transformed from a play area for games to a platform for display. Of her early teen years in the 1960s, she says, "We just wanted to be *seen* on the front porch!" Strategies for hiding out of view came later:

By the time we began to experience those first stirrings of puberty, we came to appreciate the landscaping that surrounded our porch, though not through the eye of a nature lover. On each corner of the porch there was a bush called "Bridal Wreath." . . . About four feet back, on each side of the house, there were huge azalea bushes out to the edge of the house. On the left side of the porch, this configuration provided a small area where you could not be clearly seen from the road or the front door. . . . I still remember experiencing my very first kiss in that little dark corner beside the porch. (4)

When Myra Pellowski and her sisters were finally allowed to leave the house for a date, she says that the porch "was a castle bridge, a barrier beyond which we did not step until our 'gentleman caller' had mounted the steps, knocked on the door, and provided Daddy with a 'firm' handshake and a very polite and suitable greeting" (4).

Genevieve Flynn Ross echoes the frustrations of teenagers as she recalls the difficulty in finding the necessary privacy for courting on a porch:

All the neighbors had porches, and it made for a total lack of privacy that I wonder at now, but you sure shared your life's experiences. Heaven knows at seventeen I hated it! Any date that I had was viewed with much enjoyment, curiosity, and random remarks by all the folks on the street. Like, what kind of car he had, what he looked like, how many times I dated him. . . . If your date was late . . . sigh . . . or if there were guests, and there often were, you had to introduce the poor guy to everybody there. . . . I cannot tell you how I dreaded it . . . Law . . . but looking back, I enjoy the memories of the closeness because, of course, I got to share the neighbors' lives, too, and took a total interest in everything they did. I reckon it kept a lot of us young people in line.

Ross's story again shows how the porch, with its "total lack of privacy," is a device for social control to keep "a lot of young people in line."

Such control would come not only from adults but also from other children

Grace Piner Boshamer on her porch swing, "an ideal place for courting," Morehead City, N.C., ca. 1949. (Photograph courtesy of Grace Boshamer)

who lurked in the shadows as likely tattletales. Grace Boshamer of Raleigh, North Carolina, recalls her 1930s childhood in Morehead City, a small seaport on the coast of North Carolina, where, according to Boshamer, "porches were indeed popular. I can't recall a single home without a porch." Her older siblings courted on their porch swing, and Boshamer remembers her role as the pestering, younger child: "The swing was an ideal place for courting back then. I had two older sisters, Rachel and Mattie. Rachel is nine years older, Mattie, seven years older. They often entertained their beaus sitting on the swing. I was bribed with many nickels and dimes to disappear, as I must have been a terrible nuisance. Years later I, too, entertained my beaus sitting on the same swing."

Sometimes the porch is even a training ground for young people to teach them how to behave in courtship rituals, according to decorum. Consider the following story told by Louise Kenney, a retired music teacher and guidance counselor from Lafayette, Louisiana. Kenney recalls her girlhood on her family's porch in Alexandria, where her maternal grandmother from Avoyelles Parish would often visit:

On rainy days in the fall of the year, my grandmother—sixtyish, short, and stocky—always liked to sit on our front screened porch that had a swing. This porch faced the backfield of a boys' private high school, so we liked to watch them practice their exercises and plays even in the rain. After their practice, when things became quiet and heavy rain was falling, we always seemed hungry. She liked apples and Ritz crackers and asked me to get these for us to eat while swinging and talking and laughing. I prepared a tray as well as a nine- or ten-year-old girl could, and I always wanted to please this grandmother, who somehow found the right words to praise me whether for my dress, my piano playing, or my helping around the house.

This particular day, while my parents were at our business, we ate our apples and Ritz crackers (which neither needed) until we ate the entire box.... While eating, she shared stories of her early childhood, the difficulties, and her education culminating in the seventh grade. Finally we looked at the empty tray and box, whereupon she turned to me and said, "Yes, sir, you'll make some man mighty proud the way you serve apples and Ritz crackers." Today, in 1996, after nearly 43 years married to the same man with four sons and three grandchildren, whenever it rains my thoughts always return to "that front porch" and the apples and Ritz crackers.

There are no suitors present in Kenney's story. Nevertheless, the young Louise is able to study a pack of young men as they exhibit their prowess on the football field, while at the same time she is being taught how to serve apples and Ritz crackers to potential callers. In the sensual smells of cool rain and ripe fruit, while watching the vigorous play of healthy young men, the grandmother cannot help but make an association with Louise's future marriage, a matter which is a foregone conclusion. Even today, Kenney's thoughts of marriage are intimately tied to the act of serving fruit in the cool rain on the front porch.

Kenney, as a child, does not overtly associate her porch with her emerging sexuality. The sensual imagery of her story, however, suggests her coming into her sexuality. A poem by Shannon Marquez McGuire, titled "Night-Blooming Cereus," also reveals how some children become aware, some more consciously than others, of their emerging sexuality on porches—in this case the back porch:

> The grown-ups left us watching to keep us out the way.
> Big terra cotta pots spilled Night-blooming Cereus.

The long green tubes held petaled, tumid secrets,
the seven buds as large as both my folded hands.
A sticky, dripping evening, a hot New Orleans' May.
Swinging and swinging on a porch lit by the moon.
Seven. A magic, lucky number, the number of my years.

While evening rains threw steam up from the sidewalks,
clock-watching but too young to guess at secrets unfolding
in the moonlit air, I longed for more than blossoms.
A drowsy breeze moved undulant through latched screens.
In simple pots of clay, green stems whorled serpentine.
Swinging and swinging, we children watched, forgot,
and thought to watch again those creamy desert buds.

At twelve, at last, almost too late for children's eyes,
the flowers' nodes released, like waking infants
opening their hands. Wide-eyed, I stared: The outsides
of those blossoms merely hinted at the intricate
withins. Petaled frills around their limbus,
opalescent satin roses with wool around their hearts.
A slight, corrupting sweetness moved balmy in that

porch's fanswept, moonlit air. The scent, I breathed
down to my toes and tried to hold. To learn their shape,
I spread my fingers in a circle, and pressed the fleshy
flowers of my palms. So late to bed, the next day found
me slumping over notebooks to sketch the flowers' shape.
I waited all that morning till my teacher turned away.
I closed my eyes, I wet my partly parted lips.

Softly across my tongue, I let words slip.
Over wet lips, syllables as smooth as cream:
Seven. Secret. Night-blooming Cereus. Seen.

Certainly the imagery in "Night-Blooming Cereus" is more overtly sexual than
the images of cool rain, sliced apples, and Ritz crackers in Kenney's porch story.
The speaker in this poem, a seven-year-old girl among other children on a New

Orleans back porch, waits for the cactus, a night-blooming cereus, to reveal its "intricate withins" at midnight. Longing for "more than blossoms," the girl's imagination is inflamed by the summer rain, the "drowsy breeze," the "creamy nodes" of the cactus, and by the "slight corrupting sweetness" that "moved balmy in that porch's fanswept, moonlit air." The other children seem to fade into the background as the young girl contemplates secrets that she is still "too young to guess at."

Shannon McGuire's poem and the above stories speak to the secreted impulses of a young girl on the threshold of her emerging sexuality. Some sexual uses of the porch are not nearly so inscrutable. The following humorous story, told by Andre' Brock, an LSU student, recounts a "local legend" that circulates in Reserve, Louisiana, and that has been passed down to him by his grandfather:

> There's a group of old men who always hang around in front of a small building at the corner of the two main streets in Reserve. Old men have hung out there to talk about the weather since way before I was born. There used to be a central grocery store at the site, then when I was a kid it was a full-service gas station. Now it's just an abandoned building, but I still see old men hanging out on a bench in front of it whenever I go back home.
>
> Well, here's the point of the story. My grandfather told me that this was the "DDC," or "Dead Dick Club." I've heard other people from Reserve refer to them as the same. My grandfather told me that they got this name because they all have . . . well, dead dicks. I'm sorry, but there's no polite way to say that. Now here's where my "Pappy's" originality kicks in. He claimed, and now it's well known in my family, that there was and is an initiation process to join the prestigious DDC. A prospective member (no pun intended) has to drop his drawers in front of the group. A formal inspection ensues to be sure there is no life left in said body part. One day, someone was in the middle of the initiation when a breeze blew by. The resulting movement was perceived as "life" in the unfortunate man's penis, and he was not allowed to join.

The porch here is obviously more symbolic of past sexual prowess than emerging sexual impulses. And it also is a wonderful example of how the porch can bring together a "gathering of old men," to borrow loosely from Ernest Gaines, to joke about their "golden years."

Despite their open mockery of their now-defunct sexual lives on the now-defunct store porch, the "members" of the DDC, when they did engage in courting, were probably bound by stricter courtship traditions more telling of World War II values than of post-Vietnam mores. Before World War II, courting was often done at the woman's home, as Beth Bailey's study of twentieth-century American courtship in *From Front Porch to Back Seat* confirms. Bailey traces how courtship moved from the private world of "calling" to the public world of "dating." With the advent of the automobile, young couples began to expect to leave the home to do their courting. As Bailey says: "Dating moved courtship into the public world, relocating it from family parlors and community events to restaurants, theaters, and dance halls. At the same time, it removed couples from the implied supervision of the private sphere—from the watchful eyes of family and local community—to the anonymity of the public sphere" (13). This enormous transition in romancing certainly had economic implications. When courting entered the public domain, it entered the man's world of economic control. Thus, young men without money were forced to go without dates. And young women began to relinquish the control they had over the courting process, waiting for the man's invitation.

But lest we imagine, from the above stories, that porch use has altogether disappeared, leaving young women bereft of a semiprivate place to entertain young men, I can share a contemporary story from Kenyada Corley, who is in her early twenties. As we saw in Chapter 3, Kenyada spent much of her time on her grandmother's gallery on Garrard Street in New Orleans. But her parents' home also had a porch, the porch where she got her "first kiss." Her story goes like this:

> Okay, well I got my first kiss on the front porch, and I didn't know that my mother was looking outside of the door. I was real embarrassed because she told everybody and they still tease me about that. I was practicing kissing before I kissed him, because I didn't want to do it wrong. So my sister told my mother that I had been practicing kissing, so they were waiting, looking to see if he was gonna kiss me. And he kissed me. Mama said, "If I had had a camera, it would've been a Kodak moment!"

Kenyada's story evidences the embarrassment typical of most adolescents when their parents intrude on their courting rituals. But Kenyada's parents, bolstered by the sister's evidence, were simply exercising the right to observe the goings-on of their front porch. The relaxing of social mores is noticeable in Kenyada's

Fanning the Flames

story. The mother is not trying to prevent a kiss; she seems to be watching partly out of curiosity and partly to ensure that a kiss is just a kiss.

Elizabeth Brocato, a young woman from Alexandria, Louisiana, tells an additional story of contemporary teenage romance:

> It would be safe to say that my front porch played a major role in raising me. I played endless games of truth or dare there. It was somewhere during these games on the porch that I fell in love with my first real boyfriend. . . . My parents were always real relaxed with a curfew as long as I stayed in the neighborhood, so I can't count the number of times my friends and I stayed out all night and watched the sun rise from my porch.

The rules for Elizabeth's teenage courting and socializing were relaxed by her parents, in part because of changing social mores and in part because these activities were bounded by the porch. The pressures of the neighborhood coming from without and of the parental authority coming from within were enough to keep rowdy teenagers from overstepping their boundaries, even during all-night games of truth or dare, games that led to adolescent romance.

Adult authority on the porch can even establish expectations in a dating partner, as David Veillon II, who grew up in Ville Platte, Louisiana, and now attends LSU, reports in this story about his grandmother's porch: "There was my grandmother's stamp of approval that came with the porch, as I grew older. I began to discover girls, and sitting on the swing with my grandmother gave me an image of what kind of girl I would like to meet. I figured if a girl was good enough to sit on the very swing my grandmother sat on, then she must be all right." And, in fact, David tells of bringing dates to his grandmother's swing to judge how they measured up to his grandmother's standards.

Indeed, the porch is about standards and expectations, and violating such standards can mean public humiliation, as revealed in a story told to me by Eileen Burroughs and her mother, Mary Traxler. Traxler said repeatedly in our interview that her porch in Crystal Springs, Mississippi, was "just a gathering place for young people" when her daughter, Eileen, was growing up in the 1950s. Eileen recounted one noteworthy story in particular:

> I remember when I was little we had a Halloween party. The whole house was decorated. But the front porch had the bobbing for apples. And there was one

girl in town who was kind of a tomboy. And a lot of people didn't like her. And somebody pushed her over in a tub of apples and got her all wet. And nobody would admit to it. I was 10 or 11 years old. And then when we were in college, we were all sitting on the porch and some boys got to laughing, talking about when they pushed her into the tub. That was the first time we ever knew who pushed her.

The anonymous "tomboy's" story here uncomfortably reminds us that the porch is a place of power struggles for children. In her violation of gender roles, the tomboy also violates the boys' notions of appropriate "girl" behavior, and thus she has to be punished for it. One has to wonder if the porch was ever a romantic site of heterosexual display for this girl, as it was for the other young people who felt free to gather on Traxler's porch. The tomboy's story exposes the presumptions of heterosexuality that define porch courtship and the narrow roles we construct as "masculine" and "feminine." Indeed, the tomboy's story invites our attention to the Other side of the porch to hear porch stories that are not always ratified by the larger culture.

VIOLATING BOUNDARIES

In the previous chapter, I discussed how Bone, in Dorothy Allison's *Bastard Out of Carolina*, uses her grandmother's front porch to escape the terrors of sexual abuse. But Bone's life does not end in terror. In spite of all the violations that Bone must endure, and despite her mother's unwillingness to love Bone enough to "kill [Daddy Glen] if need be" (107) in order to protect her daughter, Bone is able to seize a degree of power for herself. And she does so, in part, by using her Aunt Raylene's front porch. Raylene's porch is where Bone finds permanent safety and where she can begin to define a "white trash lesbian" identity—a "transgressive" identity that violates conventional, middle-class, heterosexual porch rituals of romance.

In order to escape Daddy Glen's violence, Bone spends a great deal of time with her Aunt Raylene while she is growing up. It is significant to Bone's emerging sexuality, though, that Raylene's porch is framed in lesbianism. Raylene herself is a lesbian, and Bone manipulates Raylene's porch territory to express her own emerging sexuality. Namely, Bone hides the metal chain with which she masturbates under Raylene's porch—on the wrong side of the porch—in order to conceal her "transgressive" sexual practices. In her collection of essays, Skin, Dorothy Allison says that she is not only a lesbian; she is a "transgressive lesbian." She says:

> [I am] femme, masochistic, as sexually aggressive as the women I seek out, and as pornographic in my imagination and sexual activities as the heterosexual hegemony has ever believed. . . . My sexual identity is intimately constructed by my class and regional background, and much of the hatred directed at my sexual preferences is class hatred—however much people, feminists in particular, like to pretend this is not a factor. The kind of woman I am attracted to is invariably the kind of woman who embarrasses respectably middle-class, politically aware lesbian feminists. My sexual ideal is butch, exhibitionistic, physically aggressive, smarter than she wants you to know, and proud of being called a pervert. Most often she is working class, with an aura of danger and an ironic sense of humor. There is a lot of contemporary lip service paid to sexual tolerance, but the fact that my sexuality is constructed within, and by, a butch/femme and leather fetishism is widely viewed with distaste or outright hatred. . . . [But] one of the strengths I derive from my class background is that I am accustomed to contempt. (23–24)

Answering to her felt contempt of "middle-class" lesbians, Allison reveals her preference for rough sex—which she sees as deeply grounded in her "white trash" background. And Bone reflects Allison's own "transgressive" preferences in the masturbation scenes with her chain. Manipulating the porch's liminality, Bone takes the chain out from under Aunt Raylene's porch and retreats to the privacy of her room for sexual experimentation. The porch, here, is certainly not used for public displays of conventional sexuality; rather, it is more private than public, providing a hiding place for Bone's "transgressions." Bone tells us: "I got in bed and put [the chain] between my legs, pulling it back and forth. It made me shiver and go hot at the same time. . . . I used the lock I had found on the river bank to fasten the chain around my hips. It felt sun-warmed and tingly against my skin. . . . It was mine. It was safe. Every link on that chain was magic in my hand" (193). While Bone, even if she were fully aware of her own lesbianism in this episode, could not participate in traditional, middle-class, heterosexual courtship rituals, she nevertheless makes use of Raylene's porch to shield her tools of sexual pleasure. She is unaware, fully, of her lesbianism. She says, "What I really wanted was not yet imagined" (193). But she is quite aware of her taste for transgressions. And the porch, framed in Raylene's lesbianism, helps her realize her unconventional preferences.

It is no wonder, then, that Raylene's porch becomes Bone's "healing porch" at the end of the novel. Indeed, the front porch is traditionally a site for emotional healing—a place to sit in peace, collect oneself, and to escape tensions from within the home. After Bone has been violently raped by Daddy Glen, and after her own mother has chosen to leave with Daddy Glen rather than to stay and protect her own daughter, Bone reflects, in a rocker on Aunt Raylene's porch, about her destiny. She says, "I was already who I was going to be. . . . When Raylene came to me, I let her touch my shoulder, let my head tilt to lean against her, trust her arm and her love. I was who I was going to be, someone like her, like Mama, a Boatwright woman. I wrapped my fingers in Raylene's and watched the night close in around us" (309). Bone might have been "born on the wrong side of the porch," but, with her fingers wrapped in Raylene's, she is ready to articulate an identity as a survivor. In order to survive, though, Bone must violate middle-class and heterosexual traditions that our culture authorizes but that have failed her so miserably. On Raylene's porch, Bone has crossed over into the safety and security of a nontraditional family and created a "space"—a "practiced place"—for herself. Raylene's porch safely situates Bone on the threshold of her emerging identity, positioning her to embrace and to affirm her own "transgressions" and to be ready to face the world on her own terms.

Repositioned for survival, Bone's future seems not only bearable but hopeful. I like to imagine the front porch of Bone's future as a "space" where she can experience the kind of loving relationship that I saw in a contemporary lesbian couple in New Orleans. In the case of Laurie Reed and Deyette Danford, the porch is a celebrated "space" for asserting their sexual identity. But first, a clarification: I am not associating "domestic abuse" with "lesbianism." Dorothy Allison herself does not make this connection. Her sisters, who also were sexually abused by their stepfather, are all heterosexual. And the gay and lesbian people I include in this chapter grew up in nurturing, loving homes. I include these Other voices in the same chapter simply because they have been constructed as just that—Other—for one reason or another.

Fanning the Flames

"OUT" ON A PORCH

Laurie and Deyette, both professional women nearing forty, met each other in 1997 while celebrating Mardi Gras at Rubyfruit Jungle, a New Orleans lesbian bar. Laurie, a social worker who holds a Master of Divinity degree from a Presbyterian seminary, and Deyette, a successful salesperson for Westlaw, have, in their time together, developed, to my mind, an enviable relationship. And the front porch of Deyette's raised-basement house in uptown New Orleans has been central to solidifying their dynamic, openly gay relationship—a relationship that could be much more open in the 1990s than in previous decades.

In Deyette's own words, this couple is "about as out as you can get," so they feel at liberty to kiss romantically on their front porch. Because Deyette's sales territory takes her out on the road, and because Laurie works in Baton Rouge during the week, the two women will go several days without seeing each other. And their weekly greetings often take place on the porch. Laurie says:

> Every time that I arrive, if the minute we see each other is on the porch, we grab each other and kiss each other, or down there [at the bottom of the steps], even, in front of the neighbors. Nobody says anything. I mean they may look, but they don't even act that interested. That's just a difference between New Orleans and Baton Rouge, really. But we actually do that even in Baton Rouge.

While Baton Rouge is somewhat conservative-minded, New Orleans has for a long time made a space for the gay community. I would imagine that some relationship exists between New Orleans's gay-friendly culture and the couple's freedom to be "out" on their porch. But Deyette, in particular, insists that even a hostile neighborhood would not stop her from using her own porch in her own way. For her, the decision to be "out" is political, even urgent. Deyette is on the board of directors of the Human Rights Campaign, the largest lesbian and gay political group in the country. She boldly says, "I'm not afraid" of stares, or hostile looks, or harassing comments. In her neighborhood, she does not have to be. There are several gay couples on their block, and their heterosexual neighbors accept their lifestyle. But I believe Deyette when she says that she would use her porch in her own way, even in a less accepting neighborhood. As she said, "Those are decisions about coming out and being who you are."

In their community of shared values, Laurie and Deyette spend their weekends together, sitting on their porch swing, making comments to passing neighbors about living "the life," volunteering to take pictures of home-loving tourists, who frequently want to pose on the steps of their porch. They occasionally host political fund-raisers, when the porch becomes a charged, deliberate public expression of the couple's sexuality. Deyette says:

> [The porch] feels private but I know that it's public as well. You know what I mean? A lot of times, and we haven't done this yet, but when we have our women's fund-raiser in November for a group I'm involved in here, we'll probably put a rainbow flag outside on the flagpole. So it really makes a statement and makes everybody feel welcome. I think that's a public display.

If porch liminality is about negotiating tensions between public and private spheres, Laurie and Deyette, because of their commitment to be out, situate their porch toward the public world. Their porch is about making their gay friends feel welcome and about openly expressing their sexuality—about moving, so to speak, from the closet to the porch.

The porch not only helps Laurie and Deyette to publicly declare their sexuality; it also helps them to define the roles in their own more private, domestic relationship. It is obvious, upon first glance, that Deyette dresses as the "butch" partner and Laurie appears to be the "femme" partner in their relationship. But the porch has allowed the couple to resist stereotypical "butch/femme" roles. Indeed, many lesbians do not want to merely repeat socially constructed "masculine" and "feminine" roles within a relationship of two women. Defining their roles is complicated by the fact that society at large tends to dichotomize, falsely, lesbians into these two categories, not allowing for the full range of possible identities and iterations. But Deyette and Laurie, while openly exhibiting a "butch/femme" relationship, are also able to resist prescribed roles.

As I said, Deyette appears to be the "butch" partner. She herself joked that she is the "poster child for 'dyke' hair," and when she wears suits and stockings to work, she claims that she is simply putting on her "work drag." Deyette appears butch because that is her preference. First, she is committed to being "as out as you can get," so her appearance is a concrete sign to others that she is a lesbian. But during our interview, Deyette showed me a picture of herself as a young "girl." I place "girl" in quotation marks because I would have assumed that the photograph was of a boy, had Deyette not been the one showing it to me as a picture of herself. Even as a child, she preferred masculine forms of dress. She even recalls dressing up as a boy in order to be attractive to another little girl. Deyette is clearly concerned with issues related to women. She simply feels more comfortable with her butch appearance. Laurie, on the other hand, dresses, as she puts it, "as a more traditional female," and she has longish blond hair and wears light makeup. Unlike Deyette, who was dressing to attract girls at a young age, Laurie did not even come into her lesbianism until her mid-twenties. Before that, she considered herself "asexual." When she attended a Presbyterian seminary in Austin, she finally was able to identify and accept who she was.

Nevertheless, the women resist stereotypical butch/femme roles, which in the past have assigned male roles to butch women, and have positioned femmes, to quote Sue-Ellen Case, as "lost heterosexuals who damage birthright lesbians by forcing them to play butch roles" (296). In their shifting roles, this couple reminds us that gender is performative, not necessarily biological. One porch story, in particular, expresses the couple's working through their shifting and performative gender roles. Not long ago, Laurie and Deyette, along with another lesbian couple, hosted the meeting of a group called Mamoo. As they put it, "[Mamoo is] a women's discussion group, a potluck thing, we get together and talk about a topic. It's a fun thing, an empowering thing." But it is not necessarily an open-invitation gathering because Laurie jokes that she "hit on Deyette" at Rubyfruit Jungle just so she could "marry into Mamoo." Deyette has been a long-time member of the group. But when it was Laurie's first time at cohosting, she found herself trying to define her territory inside this somewhat closed society of women. She said:

> I'm really pretty much of an extrovert, but this was not "my" group [and it wasn't "her" house]. I mean, I'm like slowly but surely getting to know these people. So I didn't have as much social contact or things to say. So I figured I'd greet everybody. That gave me "something to do." Deyette was in the kitchen, believe it or not [and they laugh heartily], she's in the kitchen, I know that that's hard to understand!

Laurie says that it is "hard to understand" because Deyette, the partner tagged as "butch," is in the kitchen—certainly not barefoot and pregnant—but, neverthe-less, doing the more traditional "feminine" tasks at the stove. They are not merely repeating heterosexual roles of "masculine" and "feminine" in that Laurie was also assuming a traditionally female role—that of greeting the guests. Laurie continued her story by saying:

> There was another couple who was hosting also. Probably the more shy of the two was with me on the porch, and she's a very spiritual woman, too, and she and I wanted to talk, and we were out there. And we just kind of posted ourselves on the swing. And I had Gracie out there [the dog], because people were in and out, and I was afraid she was gonna get away. So what I decided— like I said, I needed *something to do*—so I became kind of the "parking police," so to speak. So [my friend] and I started saying, "Why don't you move up just a little bit?" We were just having fun with it, telling these very independent, dyke women where to park. And they're like, "What's up here!" And it gave me a way to connect with them.

And she did connect, because several of the guests, at the end of the evening, told Deyette that they had never, with her former partner, felt so welcome at her house. As Deyette said: "This is really important, I think. Laurie is very warm, and gracious, and is more like me than this woman was like me, which is why we're not together anymore. But [a friend] made the comment to Laurie that she had never felt so welcome as she had with Laurie being on the porch and welcoming people, and a lot of people felt that way." The group of about fifty women felt free to socialize on the porch before the meeting began—some standing on the porch, some sitting on the swing, some reclining on the different levels of steps, but all defining the porch as a lesbian space. Then they all reluctantly moved inside to hold their discussion. The porch, on this evening, functioned not only to proudly exhibit the sexual orientation of the women in Mamoo; it also served as a passage to coupledom for Laurie and Deyette, helping them to gain acceptance within their community as being "together." And it is important again to note that their particular tensions here do not necessarily mirror heterosexual pressures: Their gender roles are not male/female, but, rather, those that must be defined by two women who construct their own gender roles in conversation with butch/femme dichotomies.

Laurie's and Deyette's stories tell us that discussions of the porch as a celebrated folk institution need to go beyond reporting heterosexual traditions of courtship. When we look to the Other side of the porch, our notions of "celebration" are expanded in terms of resistance, power, and diversity. Certainly, my parents' story, as well as all the others, speaks to valuable porch traditions in southern culture. But so does Laurie and Deyette's story. Their porch is an open "space," in de Certeau's sense, to resist, unapologetically, compulsory hetero-sexuality—a space where passing as straight is not only unimportant but re-pudiated.

PRIVACY, PEACE, AND SOLITUDE

But what happens when gays and lesbians do not find themselves inside a "community of shared traditions," but, rather in a less accepting environment? Recall the humiliation experienced by the tomboy who was pushed into the apple-bobbing tub, and we begin to get a clue. Or what happens if they are merely of a shyer personality than Laurie and Deyette? Some gays and lesbians are reluctant to be as "out" on the porch as Laurie and Deyette. I said earlier that New Orleans' gay-friendly culture perhaps contributes to Laurie and Deyette's ease at using their front porch to so openly express their sexuality. The story of a gay man in Baton Rouge, who prefers to be called "Doc" here, might illustrate how the local norms of a specific location, combined with a person's more conserva-tive personality, can regulate, even in a more tolerant society, the behavior of a gay man on the porch.

Baton Rouge, in its expressions of social behavior, is far more conservative than New Orleans. While Laurie and Deyette say that they are not intimidated by Baton Rouge, that they are making decisions about being out, Doc does not feel the same degree of liberty—probably because his family plays a prominent role in his hometown of Baton Rouge. The fact that he asked me to use a pseudo-nym here verifies his reluctance. This is not to say that Doc, a physician in Baton Rouge, is not out. He is. It's just that there are degrees of "outness." Doc is ac-tively involved in gay and lesbian organizations in the community. But his family has long been established in Baton Rouge, and by moderating his behavior, he is, in part, trying to protect his family from needless harassment.

The irony of Doc's situation is that he lives in Spanish Town, Baton Rouge's equivalent of the French Quarter. Spanish Town (my own neighborhood) has long been seen as gay-friendly. It is one of the few neighborhoods in Baton Rouge where gays and lesbians could conceivably express their sexuality on the front porches of their own homes. And, in fact, some do. But Doc's connection to the city at large and to his extended family, combined with his own more conservative personality, motivates him to use caution in his sexual display. The porch for him, then, is not a liminal space to communicate to the public that he is a gay man; it is, rather, a passage to the intimacy of his home's interior.

Doc recently purchased his large Spanish Town home in order to have a place for his extended family to gather. He does not have a partner to share the home with, but his several sisters and brothers, their children, and their mother (their father is deceased) come together for each and every birthday in the family, for each holiday, and then often just because they genuinely like each other's company. They could not be further from the horrors of Ruth Anne Boatwright's family. As Doc himself told me, when endorsing biological theories of homosexuality, "I was never abused. I came from a very nurtured family and we all still communicate with each other very openly and freely." Moreover, he "grew up in a very strong, Catholic, church-going, sang-in-the-choir, altar boy family."

Doc's home is a family home, then. Moreover, it bears all of the signs of an upper-middle-class family home. Doc has recently remodeled the two-story home, which has a double gallery—upstairs and downstairs. Each gallery is approximately forty feet long and ten feet wide. If Doc felt inclined to use his porch for sexual display, he certainly has ample space on which to do it. But he doesn't. Part of his motivation is that he does not want to appear "extreme" to the public at large. As he says:

> I was in Los Angeles for four years, and I hung out with the homosexual community. And I'm very concerned about [extremism]. Some people cannot live outside of that. They became so extreme in declaring their sexual orientation, to protect themselves from whatever podunk midwestern town they lived in, that if they didn't become a tattooed, obese, shaved-head, chain-wearing lesbian, they were going to be attacked. So they dressed themselves up to be as ferocious as humanly possible.

Discretion obviously defines Doc's social code and thus his use of his expansive double gallery.

Doc is further motivated to be discreet because he does not "want to exceptionalize gay people." He says that his message "has always been to address civil rights issues, in general, but especially gay and lesbian issues." Because he does not want to be exceptionalized, he never felt the need to "come out" in "a big-deal way." When he returned to Baton Rouge from Los Angeles, his "coming out" was merely to approach his mother and say, " 'You've lived here all your life, Mother. How do you think it would be best for me to approach supporting gay and lesbian issues? Do you think I should be actively involved in an organization? What would be the best way?' " He wanted and needed the endorsement of his family for his activities. And because Baton Rouge was his hometown, he wanted and needed to carry out his activities while fully considering the concerns of his family.

And part of his discretion is simply that he is middle-aged. He says: "Would I invite somebody over and ask them to come swing on the swing with me? I mean, the reason why people went out on the porch to court was because it was a 'chaperoned visit.' You couldn't leave the house, but you could have a few minutes alone. But if you would think for a minute that he was going to try to undress her on the front porch with the parents right inside—it's not gonna happen." Doc does not see the need to court on the porch because he can simply go inside his beautiful home. His circumstances are different from Laurie and Deyette's in that they are an established couple making everyday use of their porch, rather than a single person cultivating relationships on the porch. Moreover, they are committed to being "as out as you can get," while Doc moderates his being out.

When I asked Doc if he would have any qualms about openly expressing his sexuality on his porch, even in Spanish Town, he said:

A little bit. I don't know if it's my age, but I would feel weird about inviting someone over for dinner and then going out onto the front porch on the swing. Once, I openly hugged my [gay] friend on the porch, and he looked around. They look around to see if anybody is watching. My gay friends tend to be professional types of people. More conservative by nature. . . . I would not, if I were on a date, stand out on the porch and passionately kiss somebody on the front porch. Maybe it's just my conservative nature. I think it's just time to take it inside. Also, the guy who lives across the street is in my brother's office three times a week. And the neighborhood is just so volatile that I wouldn't want my personal life on the line. This place . . . you live here . . . you know how people talk in this neighborhood! I just don't want to be on the gossip line.

Indeed, Spanish Town is a small neighborhood with a very active grapevine. Police officers have told us residents that they are relieved when a crime happens in Spanish Town, rather than in another neighborhood, because people are so nosy and provide so many details that they can catch the criminal within a day or two. Doc's porch is certainly not situated as a conduit to the gossip of the neighborhood. We have seen in previous narratives how the porch can operate as what Patricia Meyer Spacks calls an "instrument of social control." In most of our stories, the porch has controlled the behavior of young people. But in Doc's story, we see that even an adult is forced to give way to the social constraints of the porch, particularly in his hometown—a socially conservative hometown at that—and particularly when the adult is gay or lesbian.

Doc's discretion does not mean than he won't make use of his double gallery as he continues his remodeling project. He has every intention of fully using it, but unlike Laurie and Deyette, who use their porch as more of a public space than a private one, Doc intends to design his porch for private use. He wants to have lawn parties at which "the porch is completely used as a social event," but, of course, the parties will be private. On the east end of the lower gallery, he intends to put a swing so that he can sit out in the morning and the evening. On the west end, he intends to enclose a space, either with blinds or shutters, so that he can have a quiet, candlelit dinner without being disturbed. He says, "I do not have a problem with somebody walking by and seeing me eating; I have a problem with a person trying to enter that environment." Clearly, Doc needs a back porch. But since he does not have one, he plans to design his "front region" to have the dynamics of a "back region."

His plans for the upper gallery are even more intimate. While he might share his private dinner space on the front porch with a guest, the upper gallery, which he calls his "balcony," will be designed solely for himself, where even his guests and dates will not be invited. He says that "a balcony is private; a porch is social." These are his plans for the upstairs gallery:

> Upstairs, I really really want the upstairs to be personal. If I were gonna court somebody, I would do it down here [in the living room, where he and I held the interview]. Upstairs is me. That's individual. I really want—my personality type is that I will go to Mexico, I will check into a resort that has eight cabanas around a central bar. Old people go there. I will go down there where they have a hammock and hide table and chairs. I will bring my medical journals. It is a luxurious place. The food is absolutely fantastic. The beach is wonderful—

right off the bar there. And I will go there for absolute solitude and peace and knowledge accumulation. It is heaven. I want my corner of the upstairs porch to be heaven. I want that. I mean, if I could put some parrots there, I would do it. I want that kind of tropical ambience that I find very, very peaceful.

Doc's plans for the upstairs gallery tell us much about him. First, his upper-middle-class status is relatively secure. His income as a physician allows him to recreate the paradise that he finds in Mexico (a universe away from the "piss scents" of Bone's front porch in South Carolina). Doc's gallery also indicates his desire for privacy, peace, and solitude. Doc's upper gallery, and even his lower gallery, are indeed entirely different spaces from the buzzing activity of porch spaces that we have seen in previous stories.

A lingering question about Doc's uses of his extravagant porch is whether or not the discrimination against gays and lesbians found in the larger culture prevents him from using his porch as an individualized, creatively used "space." Is it a "place" framed in the dominant culture's homophobia? To some extent, this must be true. Doc does not want his being gay to be part of the grapevine; if it were, it would hurt not only him but his family. However, my impression in the interview with Doc was that he is using his porch as he *prefers*, as a place of solitude and peace. If he did not prefer solitude, he would not vacation as he does — seeking out private Mexican cabanas to read his medical journals. Unlike Laurie and Deyette, he does not want to use his porch to display his sexual orientation. Nevertheless, his porches are "spaces" rather than "places," because he has the self-determination and the economic wherewithal to shape his porch to his own satisfaction, even as he is in negotiation with the community at large.

And, at the end of the day, porches have always been about — and they will always be about — self in negotiation with community. We have seen and will continue to see different iterations — grounded in prevailing social norms — of these negotiations. The stories we have looked at confirm that porches are still in use today, and they are still sites where identity politics get played out.

CONCLUSION: THE HOPE OF THINGS TO COME

The stories we have read come together, in the final analysis, to confirm that the porch is much more than a shady spot for sipping iced tea—though it certainly is that. Porches, front and back and side and other, are powerfully constructed "places," liminally situated between indoors and out, where people must work to reconcile the demands of a family, the norms of a community, and the desires of individuals—all of which are governed by a social and political context—to create an individualized "space" for themselves.

Having read so many dynamic stories from bygone eras could force a nostalgic conclusion here, in which we long for the porches of our distant past, the absence of which causes us to mourn the current state of society. However, I would like to end by looking to the future: I believe that, while television, air-conditioning, and changing lifestyles have altered the life of the porch, these factors have not destroyed its vitality. My students at Louisiana State University, alone, have convinced me that the porch is still alive for many, both in memory and in reality. I will wager that their stories are not limited to South Louisiana.

Many of my former folklore students, in journal and paper assignments, shared touching memories of porches in their lives. It is true that some of these memories speak more to the past than to the future, but as the narratives below indicate, they are nevertheless vigorous, life-shaping memories that provide a sense of hope:

My mother, before she died, always had a very close relationship with her mother, which continues with the three of us grandchildren. We spent many weekends at my grandmother's house. To us, these weekend trips were mini vacations, and we spent many hours on that porch. The floor is hardwood, which used to make sliding across it in socks tremendously fun for us. When the door that separated the porch from the rest of the house was

closed, it became a different world for Dayna, David, and me. . . . As pleasurable as the porch was during the day, it became a place of mystery at night. Darkened and closed off, it sometimes scared us as night fell. It's strange how such a place can be so magical and frightening all at the same time. . . . A lot has changed about that porch. It now holds old patio furniture, and my grandmother has put a large area rug down, which all but covers the hardwood floor. My mother once tried to convert it into a sitting room, but it was never really finished. One Christmas, not too long ago, David, Dayna, and I sat on the porch remembering when we played there as children. Although it seems a lot more desolate now, the memories are always there, floating around like mist. . . . Those summers in Rayne, Louisiana, connect me to my brother and sister, and the memories have always served to strengthen the bond we share and depend on. It's a bond my mother spent most of her life cultivating, and we would be lost without it.
—Debbie Darby

When I was young and would visit my Mawmaw and Pawpaw, his favorite space was his swing on his back porch. I remember many times when I would get up early in the morning and my Pawpaw would already be sitting on his swing with a cup of milk. The day always started with a glass of milk back there with him. Then, as I got older, I began to notice that whenever the family would get together, we always ended up on the back porch with Pawpaw sitting on his swing. It was an old wooden swing that hung right against the wall in front of the window that looked out from the kitchen and dining area. He grew tomatoes along the right side of his porch and big prickly bushes along the back. I spent many hours sitting back there talking with my Pawpaw and establishing a wonderful relationship with him. Even today, after he has been gone for over two years, I still get tears in my eyes when I see that swing or sit out there on it and look across the yard at his dogs. He taught me many things in my life. But he mostly taught me to cherish every day and everyone in my life.
—Jennifer Crawford

The years of 1980 to 1991 were special times for me. I have very fond memories of my porch. That old wooden porch at the front of my old house in Lawtell,

Louisiana. For those who don't know, Lawtell is one of the countriest places in Louisiana, and is located between Opelousas and Eunice. When I was a baby, probably one or two, I used to sit out on that old porch and mess with the chickens. I don't remember those times, but my mother always told me and my sister how we used to sit out on the porch and play with the chickens. As I got older, the porch made a great place for me to play with my G.I. Joes and Transformers, and I used to leap off the porch hoping that I would fly. The porch also made for some interesting conversations and learning experiences. Everyone knew my grandfather, and people would always come by to talk to him, and they'd sit out on the porch and speak in that old Creole French. I would sit out there with them and just listen to the way they spoke and say to myself that I'd learn French someday. . . . Yep, these were the important years to me. Mostly because of the time I got to spend with my mother. She died in 1994 when I was fourteen, and I was glad that she was there for me and never let me down. We would all just stand on that old porch like one united entity, and as long as I remember this here porch, I'll always be able to hold on to the memories.

—Shaun Guillory

My grandmother, who recently passed away, had a ramshackle little house in Bachelor, Louisiana, without air-conditioning until she was much older and her sons bought it for her. She was very reluctant to use it and would only turn it on in the most sweltering heat. My favorite memory? My grandmother was an artist. She would sit on her porch and paint the bayou in front of her. She had dozens of cats, and they would rub against her legs and the wind chimes would ring. . . . It makes me sad to think that porches might be dying out, but porches are alive and well in Bachelor. People can always be seen socializing—drinking iced tea and eating homemade gingerbread cookies. (My grandma always made me Rice Krispie Treats because those are what I liked best.)

—Brandi Moore

Some people use their porches to tell stories, some use them as a place to gather with their family, and others use them for memories. I use my porch

to help me remember all the times I have spent with my relatives who have passed away. . . . My Grandpa René died when I was thirteen years old. The most vivid memories I have with him took place on my porch. I remember a crawfish boil that took place when I was four. My Grandpa was sitting on a lawn chair next to the big crawfish pot. I remember exactly what I was wearing: turquoise shorts, a white Strawberry Shortcake shirt, red Care Bear Velcro shoes, and pigtails. I was very scared of the crawfish in the pot, so I would not go near it. I guess he noticed I was scared because he called me over to him. I remember looking in the pot and seeing tons of bright red crawfish surrounded by corn and little, red potatoes. My Grandpa then took one crawfish out of the sack and showed it to me. He told me that it was already dead, so it could not hurt me. He gave me one, too, and we played with them, making them talk to each other. Every time I sit on my porch, I am reminded of this crawfish boil.
—Monica Savoie

These tender memories of family porches help to keep alive loved ones lost to death. Many university students are beginning to face the passing of their grand-parents and some even of their parents. They are seeking ways to grieve, and remembering the porches of those who have gone helps them to cope. Such intergenerational ties with those who have passed on could make us fearful that, with the death of these students' family members, the porches of their lives also will disappear, even if memories will linger. But memories are powerful shaping forces of future choices. The affection for the porches in these stories makes me hopeful that the students will seek porches of their own in the future.

Indeed, some students have demonstrated that the porch is alive in reality as well as memory, and their accounts explicitly promise "the hope of things to come":

A place that is important to me is the back porch at my grandmother's house. It is a screened area (screened to keep the mosquitoes out), but it has a large black wrought-iron table with six black wrought-iron chairs. It also has a large fan and two large reclining chairs on the sides. We will sit out there for dessert after each meal we have there. Or if we have a shrimp, crawfish,

or crab boil, that is where we will sit and eat. We'll talk about things in the past, things we have planned, things about why I'm not out of college yet, and always politics. Lately, our President Willy has been the biggest topic. That's what that place is for me. The meeting grounds. I always imagine pounds of crawfish piled up on the table. The beer, potatoes, and corn. My grandmother complaining about the temperature. The baby running around crying, laughing, squealing, and causing general havoc. *This is a place that I never want to see go — the remembering of things past, and the hope of things to come* [emphasis added].
—Brandon Lacroix

My parents do a lot of entertaining, and the back porch is the main attraction, assuming the weather permits. They love the back porch. Every morning my father reads the paper and drinks his coffee, in his robe, on the back porch. They love to be outside. But it is my mother that does the gardening, cleaning, cooking and typical labor-intensive activities that come with the back porch. My father uses it only for relaxation or unwinding purposes. They also have a "porch relationship" with the next-door neighbors. My mother and the lady next door have done things outside of the home together, but I don't believe they have ever been in one another's homes before.
—Michelle Purvis Lazarus

The most important porch for me is that at my grandparents' house. Their house sits on top of a large hill in the Kentucky countryside. All around is family property. My grandfather was born on this farm, and his father was, too. My mother spent summers there. Fifteen years ago, my grandparents built a house on a hill, and this is where the porch is. Their house overlooks beautiful countryside and a small lake. My grandfather built a pond for us kids at the foot of the hill. So whenever we visit, my mother and I at some time will sit up on that porch and talk and talk. The porch is floored with cement, so it is always cool, especially to bare feet. These sessions with my mother helped me develop a strong relationship with her, and thus with other people. These visits have given me strong roots with my family. I have learned to appreciate my family and my family's soil.
—Kathleen Tittlebaum

In August of 1997 and again in 1999, I spent a week at my friend's vacation
home on Kingsley Lake, which is seven miles outside of Starke, Florida. . . .
During my time there, we would wake up in the morning and eat cereal on
the porch, then go swimming and ride the "Seadoos." In the afternoon, we
would sit on the porch in rocking chairs and read novels, just as a storm
was about to roll in and one could feel the cool breeze from the lake. . . . I
can remember going to sit on the porch by myself at night to contemplate
and write in my journal. . . . Kingsley Lake was a time of magic for me; I
went there during times when I truly needed to sit back and examine my life
and where I was going. It is the . . . first time I had the chance to rock on
an old porch on an August evening surrounded by my dearest friends. For
[my friend] and her family, it is this and so much more; it is a place where
generations have spent and continue to spend time together, sharing the
common bond of community that binds them all.
—Nena Villamil

There was never an important porch space in any of the places where I grew up.
The tradition pretty much starts with me. I have lived on my own in a variety
of different houses and apartments since I was seventeen, and not until I
moved into the house that I am currently living in did I realize the absolute
necessity of having a porch. There is no porch on this house, and from day
one I have come to despise the house because of that fact. A porch gives me
the feeling of extending my space beyond the indoors. I still feel comfortable and protected while sitting on a porch. Without one I feel trapped in the
house. I can't walk from the outside to the inside without a second thought.
I can't just hang out on the porch and watch the world go by. I really miss
that. At the house before this one, I had a nice porch with a couch and many
plants. My friends would come by and hang out on the porch. It made me
feel less cut off from the rest of the world. Somehow, even when I was alone,
I would feel much less alone on the porch. The next time I move, I will make
sure to get a place with a porch.
—Jana Nolan Fox

In one sentence, this last story by Jana Nolan Fox has summed up why porches
are still vital places for us: "Even when I was alone, I would feel much less alone

on the porch." And when Jana married and moved to Athens, Georgia, she did, in fact, move to a house with a porch.

The following story by Carmen Matthews Lavergne, another former student, echoes the comfortable privacy of a porch. Carmen's mother moved a shotgun house from Spanish Town, near downtown Baton Rouge, to Prairieville, a rural community on the outskirts of Baton Rouge, in 1960. Because the house now "sits alone on four acres of land," the family no longer experiences a sense of neighborhood. In fact, Carmen's mother "hardly knows her neighbors at all." Carmen's mother works full-time and has little time to enjoy "the leisure of the front porch." But Carmen continues by saying:

> Although the significance of the porch in our lives has decreased and the niche that it does occupy is vastly different from the historically social role that the porch has played, the porch still reflects some of the same qualities. I have always used my mom's porch as sort of a retreat when I wanted peace and quiet. Because our porch is so rarely used, no one thinks to look for me there. I have used the porch most often to think and to study. It has been for me a place of great achievement. In the seventh grade, I memorized the Preamble of the Constitution while sitting on that porch. For me, the meaning of the front porch has been transformed from a place of socialization and display to a place of peace and solitude.

Even if the porch is not a bustling place of socializing in this story, Carmen has made use of this vital space. Her intent there was to find privacy, not company. And perhaps "the hope of things to come" will mean that the porch is more about individuality than about community, given the changing nature of our everyday lives. But finding "a place of peace and solitude" is, yet and still, a fitting use of the porch.

Elizabeth Brocato, a former student from Alexandria, Louisiana, has contributed the following story about how the peace and solitude of her front porch saved her on a night of unimaginable shock and grief:

> I remember one night particularly well. Mom was home, but Dad was in Arizona for the weekend. My sister was off doing something somewhere. To remedy my boredom, I decided to go visit my boyfriend, Scott. If I had known

the outcome of the night, I never would have left. To make a long story short, Scott accidentally shot himself in the head at point blank range with a sawed-off twelve-gauge shotgun while I watched helplessly. After all of the confusion that followed, the minister volunteered to drive me home.

When we reached the house, I went inside, and Reverend Mangum followed me. I remember my grandparents' coming over, my mom freaking out, and my sister being there. My dad was called, and everyone was trying to talk to me. But I just wanted to be alone. So I went out on the porch and told them not to follow me.

I just sat there in disbelief, swinging until my nerves calmed enough to feel. Reverend Mangum eventually came outside and handed me my senior class ring and walked back inside. It was the ring that Scott had been wearing. I guess that finally made it real. I sat there holding that ring and crying at the pain my body was finally allowing me to feel. The porch, without all the sympathetic glances and hushed conversation, had provided the comfort and reality check I needed to keep from losing my mind that night.

When I look back at it now, years later, I know it was the sound of the grating metal and the gentle, predictable motion of the swing that comforted me. In a time of need like that, all I wanted was something constant, gentle, and predictable. To this day, I don't know that one person could have given me that.

Even when we are confronting unspeakable tragedies, Elizabeth's story confirms that a porch of our own can be a "constant, gentle, and predictable" space of healing. It can even be a place of spiritual revelation for those who are inclined.

LaTrista Funches, an African American student at LSU who grew up in Jackson, Mississippi, composed a touching essay about her grandmother's porch, titling her work "The Porches That Shaped Lives." She recounts how her grandmother's front porch has been, for her family, a place to find spiritual strength to face hardships. When her uncle passed away, LaTrista took up this family tradition, to find her own strength for her family:

I sat on that porch and wondered how to be strong because I didn't feel I could do it. I have never been the strongest link for our family. Then I thought of my uncle and how he was strong for everyone and how I had no other choice but to be whatever my family needed, not because I was the oldest or wisest, but because I was the strongest at this moment. Sitting on that porch, I realized you don't have to be strong all the time; you just have to be what God wants you to be on His time. Sitting on that porch brought back memories of how generations of our family have stuck together and survived because there was always something or someone that kept the family close. It was on this porch that memories of life were made. . . . You see, old traditions never die; they just fade into the air until Heaven's ready to bring them down again.

Perhaps the understanding of the porch's healing and, for some, spiritual powers is why some urban planners are reviving it in new housing designs. An article that appeared in a 1998 issue of *Environment and Behavior* explains how "New Urbanists" are seeking to restore the notion of "community" to urban dwelling areas through the use of narrower roads, sidewalks, street trees, and front porches. The authors of the article, titled "Neighbors, Households, and Front Porches: New Urbanist Community Tool or Mere Nostalgia" performed a study in which they examined the use of the porch in the years subsequent to 1920 and 1986, years when advances in technology could either favor or discourage porch use, respectively. After evaluating 272 completed interviews, the authors found that in 1920 the porch was ranked second in the category of "where sociability occurs" out of a possible eleven sites; in 1986, the porch was ranked fourth—a decent showing. The authors confirm the tendency, though, that has just been made apparent in my students' porch stories: "More spacious and comfortable homes attract more family use, as family rooms become more popular in recent times, and streets, sidewalks, and porches decline in importance as a contact site." Nevertheless, the porch in contemporary accounts proved useful to individuals and families seeking more private uses. The authors conclude:

For the individual, the front porch provides a good place to be alone and supports a number of pleasurable activities one can do alone, such as watching the neighborhood, reading a book, or enjoying nature. For households, the porch provides a site for sibling interaction; parent interaction; parent-child interaction; and interaction among neighbors, friends, and family members. Porches can support and enhance not just neighborhood cohesion but much prized leisure time for individuals and families.

The authors caution New Urbanists to include the individual, private benefits of the porch as well as those benefits related to community cohesion (Brown et al. 8).

Such advice can be salutary instruction for us all. Should we dismiss the porch because it has become more individualized and private in our contemporary society? In a world where peace and quiet are prized commodities and where families have to struggle to even sit together for a meal, the porch can contribute to our well-being by offering a space for quiet reflection and for intimate family conversations. Our neighbors are not so interested in who we date anymore; our work rarely takes place in the fields behind our house; and television and air-conditioning beckon us inside. Perhaps the future of the porch necessitates its flowing from the interior of the house that produces it, not out toward the community that surrounds it. Perhaps just knowing that the community is out there, but not in our faces, can help us to know that even when we are alone, we will feel, as Jana Nolan Fox said, "much less alone" on the porch.

"MUCH LESS ALONE"

I want to end this book with a look at two very contemporary porches in Baton Rouge. One is a porch being used at a halfway house for mentally ill women; another belongs to a software development company. Both are miles away, literally and figuratively, from the agrarian, rural uses of the porch that comprise our nostalgic memories, as so vividly recorded in this book. Both porches, in keeping with contemporary needs, mediate between the enduring need to connect with a community and the present need to gain more privacy.

The Women's Community Rehabilitation Center (WCRC) in Baton Rouge sponsors the "UpLifted" program, which helps to reintegrate mentally ill women into the world of work and home. Ever since September 1974, when the center began its work, this remarkable program has been providing supervised housing, intensive counseling, group and individual therapy, transportation, job placement, educational services, drug surveillance services, recreation services, savings and finance counseling, and follow-up services to about fifteen women at a time. And since 1976, when the facility moved to a new location in downtown Baton Rouge, WCRC has been providing the women it houses with a front porch.

I came to notice these women on my daily drives home from LSU. As I drove past the house, I would see them sitting, every afternoon, on the porch; they would occasionally wave; and I would always wonder what their story was. In my interview with several of them on June 23, 1999, I learned that their story is about healing and recovery and that this porch at the WCRC positions them to look toward the day when they are independent again.

To be admitted to the WCRC, women must have been diagnosed with either emotional disturbance or with substance-abuse problems so severe that their daily living is impaired. All of the women are over eighteen, and they have entered the program voluntarily. The goals of the WCRC are to provide a homelike atmosphere to help the women become self-sufficient in employment, social and personal relationships. The women are required to follow a set of rules and regulations, which involve regular hours of rising, eating, grooming, cleaning, and sleeping. But they are also given a certain amount of freedom during the day. Many of them choose to sit on the porch during these hours.

At a basic level, they use the porch to smoke, since the indoor facility is non-smoking. But the women also use it for social and psychological purposes. One woman said that she was "the first one out in the morning" so that she could do her daily meditation. Another woman said that she looked out to the traffic and that she was "watching where we're going." The house, situated at the foot of Interstate 10, gives view to hundreds of automobiles, with people going to and from their daily work. The women look out at the people and the automobiles, and they imagine themselves participating in such daily rituals. Their own cars cannot be used until they attain a certain level of advancement in the program, and even then the keys are kept at the front office. The cars they watch are not simple objects of curiosity; they are symbols of mobility and freedom.

The women seemed to show a deep appreciation for the WCRC; nevertheless, there are inevitable moments when they long to escape, and the porch helps to ease their feelings of confinement. They are, as one woman said, "penned up in a house with fifteen personalities." To "get away from it all," they go to the porch for some privacy. If one resident wants to tell another resident something private, she'll say, "Come on, gotta tell you something. Let's go to the porch." Especially interesting is that the WCRC offers a lovely, private patio in the backyard, but hardly any of the women use it. The patio is a place for crawfish boils, but they all said that as soon as they are finished eating, they move to the front porch. The patio is available to them when they are being "punished"; but the porch is not.

Earlier, we read of the porch as being a site of punishment for children; here, not having access is the punishment. One woman said, "The patio is really punishment." Another said, "On the patio, all we have to look at is each other." What they are seeking on the porch is less isolation, to be "much less alone" than on the patio or indoors.

But they want to see without necessarily being seen. They are, after all, at the WCRC because of special circumstances, and their privacy is highly valued. I did not even ask their names in the interview, and I collected their signed permission forms in a group, rather than from the hands of each person, to ensure confidentiality. Because they are seeking anonymity, even in the face of being "much less alone," many of the women prefer the porch late at night, after dark, when they can, with greater assurance, see without being seen. If the porch, for decades, was about seeking a personal connection with the community, this porch is about seeking a more furtive connection—to spy without being spied upon.

The WCRC porch is an integral part of the healing these various women are experiencing. Their porch provides a paradoxical use: it at once makes them feel "much less crowded" but "much less alone." By situating themselves in this liminal position—neither crowded nor alone—they find a "space" to temporarily insert themselves into the world at large, while being able to retreat to the indoors for the help and support they need to reenter that world.

If they are lucky, these women might one day find themselves working at a company that shares the philosophy of Sophcom, a software development company located in Baton Rouge. I came to know the people at this company through a student, Kelli Eskins, who took a fieldwork class with me in the fall of 1999. Kelli, a nontraditional student who has returned to the university after spending many years in the work force, prepared her final paper, which she titled "Feels Like Home: The Embodiment of Corporate Philosophy in a Porch," to pay tribute to how the porch at her workplace has helped to create a remarkable sense of family among the employees and their employers. She invited me to attend Sophcom's Thanksgiving dinner, held annually on the porch, so that I could witness for myself the distinctiveness of this corporate culture.

Sophcom was founded in 1986, when its owners, James Machen and David Kern, decided to join their talents to produce a "high-tech software company which reflects their personal values of family, character, and strong work ethic"

(Sophcom brochure). James, a thirty-something African American male who spent part of his childhood in the North, and David, a thirty-something white male from South Louisiana, have partnered to create at Sophcom a work environment so appealing that in the fourteen years they have been in business they have lost only three employees, only one of whom left by choice. This company, because of its genuine concern for its employees, would be special even without a porch. But their having a porch only makes the setting that much more of a "home."

The office building is located on the first and second floors of a twenty-year-old building. Each floor has a front gallery, but it is the upstairs gallery, complete with a handmade cypress swing, that gets used by the employees. The porch is a ten-by-thirty-foot rectangle with a painted wooden floor. According to Kelli, the swing is a recent addition. Before it was purchased, the company discussed for several months what should be chosen, and once the choice was made, there was a "ceremonial hanging, followed by an official testing ritual, attended by all" (Eskins 11; all quotes come from this essay, with the full permission of all informants). The swing quickly became the "thinking swing" for the employees. One employee said, "Whenever I get stressed out, angry at coworkers, or just plain tired, I go and sit. It enables me to relax and cool off on the swing. Sometimes when I need to do some hard thinking about a project or problem I am having, I go sit on the swing so that I can be alone with my thoughts. Sometimes people just need a little time alone" (11). Giving their employees the privacy to swing, to think—even to sleep on the swing if necessary—is what gives the business the feeling of home. Both James and David told me that they simply trusted their employees to get their work done and that they did not hire people whom they could not trust to that degree. The employees have lived up to such expectations.

James and David also trust their employees to bring their children to work. According to Kelli, "Children are an integral, everyday part of the Sophcom family. It is a rare day when there isn't at least one child on the premises, and usually there are several" (10). In addition to a "Learning Lab" that has been set up for the children, the porch is central to them. It "serves as a playhouse, a study center, and a gathering place. Crying babies are rocked on the swing, or distracted by the leaves moving in the breeze. Toddlers practice walking up and down the stairs and test limits by determining exactly how long they can lean against the iron railing before they are taken inside" (10).

James Machen (left) and David Kern (right) distributing Christmas presents at Sophcom party, Baton Rouge, La. (Photograph by Kelli Eskins, 1998)

Sophcom employee sleeping on swing. (Photograph by Kelli Eskins, 1998)

When the Sophcom family socializes on the porch, the owners prepare traditional South Louisiana meals. The Thanksgiving dinner I participated in included catfish fillets fried in a gigantic black iron skillet over a butane burner. Kelli says, "There are many jokes about the manly nature of the cooking being done, but these jibes contain an element of truth. Each of these meals requires an array of specialized utensils and implements, some of them too heavy for the average woman to lift" (8). Such was the case with the black iron skillet, which was probably about three feet in diameter. Eating can be followed by dancing on the porch. Kelli tells the following story:

> One of my favorite memories of dancing on the porch comes from a recent Thanksgiving dinner. Toward the end of the evening, I saw David Kern holding his two-year-old daughter while dancing with James Machen's twelve-year-old daughter, Leah. It has become a tradition that Sophcom is the place where

Conclusion

Sophcom family: Kelli Eskins standing next to David Kern, behind swing.
(Photograph by Jon Griffin Donlon, 2000)

our children learn to dance. This is particularly important for my son, whose hopes of learning to dance are quite low if they rest solely on the shoulders of a father who feels that "The Bump" is a classic dance that will suffice in any situation and a mother who grew up white, Baptist, and rhythm-impaired. I've watched him follow James or Dave, carefully mimicking every move they make, including an inadvertent nose-scratch, which he interpreted as a styl-ized hand gesture. (9)

James Machen's childhood experiences of dancing on his grandmother's porch have, in part, led to this corporate tradition. He told Kelli that as children they would "toss some sawdust on the floor—that way you can get that whole slide action thing going" (9). Bringing family traditions onto the porch of the work-place has certainly contributed to the distinct corporate culture of home.

Conclusion

And perhaps Sophcom can speak to the future of the American porch, to "the hope of things to come." If present-day work takes whole families out of the home, then perhaps a porch swing on site can help employees to recover what has been lost. Certainly we can all learn lessons from Sophcom about using porches as a place to break down boundaries of race, gender, and class, to create a sense of family and community that includes children, and to provide a space for daily meditation when the world is too much with us. Sophcom represents a twenty-first century model for using porches that accommodate our changing culture's need for privacy while embracing traditions of home and community.

In her most recent novel, *Divine Secrets of the Ya-Ya Sisterhood*, Rebecca Wells laments the disappearance of the porch. Remembering a time when the women who comprised the Ya-Ya Sisterhood spent their childhood on a house porch, the narrator tells us:

> You could not put your finger on it, but you knew these women shared secret lagoons of knowledge. Secret codes and lore and lingo stretching back into that fluid time before air conditioning dried up the rich, heavy humidity that used to hang over the porches of Louisiana, drenching cotton blouses, beads of sweat tickling the skin, slowing people down so the world entered them in an unhurried way. A thick stew of life that seeped into the very blood of people, so that eccentric, languid thoughts simmered inside. Thoughts that would not come again after porches were enclosed, after the climate was controlled, after all windows were shut tight, and the sounds of the neighborhood were drowned out by the noise of the television set. (80)

It is true that such thoughts—of days gone by when the treacherous southern heat led to hours of languishing on the porch, hours that were more compulsory than voluntary—may "not come again." But the porch stories in this final chapter—of young people longing to sustain family traditions, of contemporary workplaces breaking down boundaries, of those in need seeking a place to heal, of harried individuals finding peace and solitude while being "much less alone"—all these stories and the many more still to be told indicate that new thoughts and new stories may yet provide our "hope of things to come" for the celebrated porches of the South.

WORKS CONSULTED

Afolabi Ojo, G. J. "Traditional Yoruba Architecture." *African Arts* 1.3 (1967): 14+.

Alford, Dorothy M. Letter to the author. Baton Rouge, Louisiana, September 1996.

Allison, Dorothy. *Bastard Out of Carolina*. New York: Plume Contemporary Fiction, 1993.

Arsenault, Raymond. "The End of the Long Hot Summer: The Air Conditioner and Southern Culture." *Journal of Southern History* 50 (1984): 597–628.

Aurit, Phil, Jr. Foreword to *The Front Porch: A Collection of McManus Family Memories and Recipes*, by Susan G. McManus and Jane McManus Schoen. N.p.: n.p., 1995. 5–6.

Babin, Joyce Hebert. Letter to the author. Gonzales, Louisiana, September 22, 1996.

Bailey, Beth L. *From Front Porch to Back Seat: Courtship in Twentieth-Century America.* Baltimore: Johns Hopkins University Press, 1988.

Bakhtin, Mikhail M. "Discourse in the Novel." In *The Dialogic Imagination: Four Essays.* Ed. Michael Holquist. Trans. Caryl Emerson and Michael Holquist. Austin: University of Texas Press, 1981. 259–422.

Bartlett, Joe (Bro Joe). Personal interview. Lake Charles, Louisiana, September 27, 1997.

Beckham, Sue Bridwell. "The American Front Porch: Women's Liminal Space." In *Making the American Home: Middle-Class Women and Domestic Material Culture: 1840–1940.* Ed. Marilyn Ferris Motz and Pat Browne. Bowling Green, Ky.: Bowling Green State University Popular Press, 1988. 69–89.

Bhabha, Homi K. *The Location of Culture.* New York: Routledge, 1994.

Bolsterli, Margaret Jones. *Born in the Delta: Reflections on the Making of a Southern White Sensibility.* Knoxville: University of Tennessee Press, 1991.

Boshamer, Grace Piner. Letter to the author. Raleigh, North Carolina, September 19, 1999.

Breazeale, Penny. Personal interview. New Orleans, Louisiana, September 24, 1997.

Brocato, Elizabeth. Student journal. Louisiana State University, Baton Rouge, November 1996.

Brock, Andre'. E-mail communication. December 7, 1999.

Brooks, Peter. *Reading for the Plot: Design and Intention in Narrative.* New York: Vintage, 1985.

Brown, Barbara, et al. "Neighbors, Households, and Front Porches: New Urbanist Community Toll or Mere Nostalgia?" *Environment and Behavior* 30 (1998): 579+. Also available on Internet through InfoTrac (October 10, 1998): 1–14.

Burrison, John A., ed. *Storytellers: Folktales and Legends from the South*. Athens: University of Georgia Press, 1989.

Burroughs, Eileen. Personal interview. Baton Rouge, Louisiana, July 15, 1996.

Caillouet, Elida. Letter to the author. Baker, Louisiana, September 21, 1996.

Callahan, John F. *In the African-American Grain: Call-and-Response in Twentieth-Century Black Fiction*. 2nd ed. Middletown, Conn.: Wesleyan University Press, 1989.

Carr, David. *Time, Narrative, and History*. Studies in Phenomenology and Existential Philosophy. Ed. James M. Edie. Bloomington: Indiana University Press, 1986.

Carriere, June Chachere. Personal interview. Opelousas, Louisiana, June 23, 1999.

Case, Sue-Ellen. "Toward a Butch-Femme Aesthetic." In *The Lesbian and Gay Studies Reader*. Ed. Henry Abelove, Michèle Aina Barale, and David M. Halperin. New York: Routledge, 1993. 294–306.

Cash, W. J. *The Mind of the South*. New York: Vintage, 1941.

Cavanaugh, Michael. Personal interview. Baton Rouge, Louisiana, July 10, 1996.

Coleman, Nell. Personal interview. Houma, Louisiana, July 26, 1996.

Corley, Kenyada. Personal interview. Baton Rouge, Louisiana, June 28, 1997.

Crawford, Jennifer. Student journal. Louisiana State University, Baton Rouge, November 1998.

Daigle, Renee Coleman. Personal interview. Baton Rouge, Louisiana, July 26, 1996.

Danford, Deyette. Personal interview. New Orleans, Louisiana, October 18, 1997.

Daniels, Kate. "Porch-Sitting and Southern Poetry." In *The Future of Southern Letters*. Ed. Jefferson Humphries and John Lowe. New York: Oxford University Press, 1996. 61–71.

Darby, Debbie. "My Grandmother's Porch." Unpublished student essay. Louisiana State University, Baton Rouge, October 11, 1999.

Dauterive, Henry. Personal interview. New Iberia, Louisiana, June 19, 1999.

Davis, Thadious M. *Faulkner's 'Negro': Art and the Southern Context*. Southern Literary Studies. Ed. Louis D. Rubin Jr. Baton Rouge: Louisiana State University Press, 1983.

De Certeau, Michel. *The Practice of Everyday Life*. Trans. Steven Rendall. Berkeley: University of California Press, 1984.

Dégh, Linda. *American Folklore and the Mass Media*. Folklore Today. Ed. Linda Dégh. Bloomington: Indiana University Press, 1994.

Denton, John H. "Perspectives on Race and Property." In *Race and Property*. Ed. John H. Denton. Berkeley, Calif.: Diablo Press, 1964. 3–15.

Deshotels, Leon. Personal interview. Mansura, Louisiana, July 23, 1996.

Dillard, J. L. *Black English: Its History and Usage in the United States*. New York: Random House, 1972.

"Doc." Personal interview. Baton Rouge, Louisiana, September 12, 1997.

Dorson, Richard M. *American Negro Folktales*. Bloomington: Indiana University Press, 1958.

Works Consulted

Duplantis, Karen Marie Hazelwood. E-mail communication, March 13, 2000.

Edwards, Jay. "The Complex Origins of the American Domestic Piazza-Veranda-Gallery." *Material Culture: Journal of the Pioneer America Society* 21.2 (1989): 3–58.

———. "The Evolution of Vernacular Architecture in the Western Caribbean." *Cultural Tradition and Caribbean Identity: The Question of Patrimony*. Ed. S. Jeffrey K. Wilkerson. Gainsville: Center for Latin American Studies, University of Florida, 1980. 291–332.

Ellison, Ralph. *Shadow and Act*. 1953. New York: Vintage, 1972.

Eskins, Kelli Fitzhenry. "Feels Like Home: The Embodiment of Corporate Philosophy in a Porch." Unpublished student paper, October 22, 1999.

Faulkner, William. *Absalom, Absalom!* 1936. New York: Vintage, 1987.

———. *The Sound and the Fury*. 1929. New York: Vintage, 1954.

Felski, Rita. "Nothing to Declare: Identity, Shame, and the Lower Middle Class." *PMLA* 115 (2000): 33–45.

Fontenot, Emily. Student journal. Louisiana State University, Baton Rouge, April 1999.

Foucault, Michel. *Power/Knowledge: Selected Interviews and Other Writings, 1972–1977*. Ed. Colin Gordon. Trans. Colin Gordon, Leo Marshall, John Mepham, and Kate Soper. New York: Pantheon, 1980.

———. "Space, Power, and Knowledge." *The Foucault Reader*. Ed. Paul Rabinow. Trans. Christian Hubert. New York: Pantheon, 1984. Reprinted in *The Cultural Studies Reader*. Ed. Simon During. New York: Routledge, 1993. 161–69.

Fox, Jana Nolan. Student journal. Louisiana State University, Baton Rouge, November 1998.

Frankenberg, Ruth. *The Social Construction of Whiteness: White Women, Race Matters*. Minneapolis: University of Minnesota Press, 1993.

Frazier, E. Franklin. *The Negro Church in America*. 1963. New York: Schocken Books, 1974.

Funches, LaTrista. Student journal. Louisiana State University, Baton Rouge, October 1999.

Furby, Mattie Lou Faroldo. Letter to the author. Alexandria, Louisiana, October 18, 1996.

Gaines, Ernest. *Catherine Carmier*. 1964. Chatham, N.J.: Chatham Bookseller, 1972.

Gallagher, Lillie Petit. Letter to the author. Baton Rouge, Louisiana, September 1996.

Gates, Henry Louis, Jr. *The Signifying Monkey: A Theory of African-American Literary Criticism*. New York: Oxford University Press, 1988.

Genovese, Eugene D. " 'Rather Be a Nigger Than a Poor White Man': Slave Perceptions of Southern Yeomen and Poor Whites." In *Toward a New View of America: Essays in Honor of Arthur C. Cole*. Ed. Hans L. Trefousse. New York: Burt Franklin and Co., 1977. 79–96.

Glassie, Henry. *Folk Housing in Middle Virginia: A Structural Analysis of Historic Artifacts*. Knoxville: University of Tennessee Press, 1975.

Goffman, Erving. *The Presentation of Self in Everyday Life*. New York: Doubleday, 1959.

Goldfield, David R. *Black, White, and Southern: Race Relations and Southern Culture, 1940 to the Present*. Baton Rouge: Louisiana State University Press, 1990.

Greenbie, Barrie B. *Spaces: Dimensions of the Human Landscape*. New Haven, Conn.: Yale University Press, 1981.

Greenblatt, Stephen. "Culture." In *Critical Terms for Literary Study*. Eds. Frank Lentricchia and Thomas McLaughlin. Chicago: University of Chicago Press, 1990. 225–32.

Griffith, Theresa Haydel. Letter to the author. La Beau, Louisiana, September 1996.

Guillory, Shaun. Student journal. Louisiana State University, Baton Rouge, November 1999.

Gurganus, Allan. *White People: Stories and Novellas*. New York: Ballantine, 1990.

Harris, Trudier. "Black Writers in a Changed Landscape, since 1950." In *The History of Southern Literature*. Ed. Louis D. Rubin Jr. Baton Rouge: Louisiana State University Press, 1985. 566–77.

———. *The Power of the Porch: The Storyteller's Craft in Zora Neale Hurston, Gloria Naylor, and Randall Kenan*. Athens: University of Georgia Press, 1996.

Hazelwood, Marie Foreman. Telephone interview, July 25, 1997.

Heath, Shirley Brice. *Ways with Words: Language, Life, and Work in Communities and Classrooms*. New York: Cambridge University Press, 1983.

Heitman, Danny. "Stories They Told on the Front Porch: Author Researches 'Room's' Role in Southern Culture." *Advocate* (Baton Rouge, La.), September 21, 1996. B1+.

Hemenway, Robert E. *Zora Neale Hurston: A Literary Biography*. Urbana: University of Illinois Press, 1980.

Herskovits, Melville J. *The Myth of the Negro Past*. 1941. Boston: Beacon Press, 1990.

Hodges, Frenchy Jolene. "Belle Isle (Central Park of Detroit)." In *Piece De Way Home*. Detroit: Tibi Productions, 1975. 5–9.

Holloway, Joseph E., ed. *Africanisms in American Culture*. Bloomington: Indiana University Press, 1990.

Holloway, Karla F. C. *The Character of the Word: The Texts of Zora Neale Hurston*. Contributions in Afro-American and African Studies 102. Westport, Conn.: Greenwood Press, 1987.

Hooks, Bell. *Talking Back*. Boston: South End Press, 1989.

Hurston, Zora Neale. *Dust Tracks on a Road: An Autobiography*. 1942. 2nd ed. Urbana: University of Illinois Press, 1984.

———. *Their Eyes Were Watching God*. 1937. New York: Harper and Row, 1990.

Jackson, C. Jean. Letter to the author. Baton Rouge, Louisiana, October 22, 1996.

Johnson, Barbara. "Metaphor, Metonymy and Voice in *Their Eyes Were Watching God*." In *Black Literature and Literary Theory*. Ed. Henry Louis Gates Jr. New York: Methuen, 1984. 205–19.

Johnson, Gloria. Personal interview. Lake Charles, Louisiana, May 29, 1995.

Jones, Crystal. Personal interview. New Orleans, Louisiana, September 24, 1997.

Jones, Nina W. "It's Not Just a Porch Swing, It's a Memory." In *Platinum Record*. A Publication of the East Baton Rouge Council on Aging, April 1996. 17.

Kenny, Louise B. Letter to the author. Lafayette, Louisiana, September 26, 1996.

Kirvin, Sharra. Student journal. Louisiana State University, Baton Rouge, April 1999.

Kniffen, Fred B. "Louisiana House Types." *Annals of the Association of American Geographers* 26 (1936): 179–93.

Kraemer, Liz. Letter to the author. Vacherie, Louisiana, September 21, 1996.

Labanca, Lindsay. Student journal. Louisiana State University, Baton Rouge, 1997.

Labov, William. *Language in the Inner City: Studies in the Black English Vernacular*. Philadelphia: University of Pennsylvania Press, 1972.

Lacroix, Brandon. Student journal. Louisiana State University, Baton Rouge, November 1998.

Lavergne, Carmen Matthews. Student journal. Louisiana State University, Baton Rouge, April 1997.

Lazarus, Michelle Purvis. Student journal. Louisiana State University, Baton Rouge, March 1997.

Lithgoe, Frances. Letter to the author. Baton Rouge, Louisiana, September 1996.

McGuire, Shannon. "Night-Blooming Cereus." Unpublished poem, 1990.

———. Telephone interview, May 17, 1995.

McManus, Susan. Personal interview. Baton Rouge, Louisiana, October 11, 1996.

McWhorter, Amie. Student journal. Louisiana State University, Baton Rouge, December 1999.

Major, Emma H. Letter to the author. Baton Rouge, Louisiana, September 1996.

"Man's Porch Is His Castle, A." *The Economist* (August 29, 1998): 31.

Markwith, Vivien E. Letter to the author. Colonial Beach, Viriginia, September 14, 1999.

Martin, Edith Mewborn. Letter to the author. Snow Hill, North Carolina, August 18, 1999.

Massey, Doreen. *Space, Place, and Gender*. Minneapolis: University of Minnesota Press, 1994.

Mauck, Sally Bradford. Letter to the author. Columbus, Mississippi, September 1996.

Mbiti, John S. *African Religions and Philosophy*. New York: Doubleday, 1969.

Meese, Elizabeth. "Orality and Textuality in *Their Eyes Were Watching God*." In *Crossing the Double-Cross: The Practice of Feminist Criticism*. Chapel Hill: University of North Carolina Press, 1986. Reprinted in *Modern Critical Interpretations: Zora Neale Hurston's "Their Eyes Were Watching God*." New York: Chelsea House, 1987. 59–71.

Mercer, Ottie Hazelwood. Personal interview. Baton Rouge, Louisiana, October 25, 1997.

Moore, Brandi. Student journal. Louisiana State University, Baton Rouge, November 1998.

Moore, Charles W., Kathryn Smith, and Peter Becker, eds. *American Domestic Vernacular Architecture: Home Sweet Home.* New York: Rizzoli International Publications, 1983.

Morrison, Toni. *Playing in the Dark: Whiteness and the Literary Imagination.* Cambridge, Mass.: Harvard University Press, 1992.

Naylor, Gloria. *Mama Day.* New York: Vintage, 1988.

Nelson, Dana D. *The Word in Black and White: Reading "Race" in American Literature, 1638–1867.* New York: Oxford University Press, 1992.

Noble, Allen G. *Wood, Brick and Stone: The North American Settlement Landscape.* Vol. 1, *Houses.* Amherst: University of Massachusetts Press, 1984.

Oszuscik, Phillippe. "Passage of the Gallery and Other Caribbean Elements from the French and Spanish to the British in the United States." *P.A.S.T.* 15 (1992): 1–14.

Out on a Porch: An Evocation in Words and Pictures. Introduction by Reynolds Price. Chapel Hill, N.C.: Algonquin Books, 1992.

Pellowski, Myra. "Just Three Steps and a Concrete Slab." Unpublished student essay. Louisiana State University, Baton Rouge, October 5, 1999.

Personal Narrative Group. *Interpreting Women's Lives: Feminist Theory and Personal Narratives.* Bloomington: Indiana University Press, 1989.

Philips, John Edward. "The African Heritage of White America." In *Africanisms in American Culture.* Ed. Joseph E. Holloway. Bloomington: Indiana University Press, 1990. 225–39.

Phillips, Ulrich Bonnell. *Life and Labor in the Old South.* Boston: Little, Brown and Co., 1929.

Platte, Frankie. Letter to the author. Baton Rouge, Louisiana, September 27, 1996.

Reed, John Shelton. "Carolina Couch Controversy: Local Busybodies Target the Front Porch." *Reason* (March 1998): 50–51.

Reed, Laurie. Personal interview. New Orleans, Louisiana, October 18, 1997.

Rippolo, Sindee. Telephone interview, July 9, 1996.

Ross, Genevieve Flynn. Letter to the author. Baton Rouge, Louisiana, September 1996.

Sadler, Lynn Veach. "Of Swings Deaf and Mute But Not Dumb." Unpublished essay, September 28, 1999.

St. Romain, Rose Anne. Personal interview. Mansura, Louisiana, December 11, 1997.

Savoie, Monica. Student journal. Louisiana State University, Baton Rouge, November 15, 1999.

Schoen, Jane McManus. Personal interview. Baton Rouge, Louisiana, October 11, 1996.

Shank, Rebecca Gentry. "Mother's Front Porch." *Country Almanac* (Summer 1990): 28.

Simpson, Leah Beth. Letter to the author. Amite, Louisiana, September 23, 1996.

Smith, Lee. *Oral History.* New York: Ballantine, 1983.

Soja, Edward. "History: Geography: Modernity." In *Postmodern Geographies: The Reassertion of Space in Critical Social Theory.* London: Verso, 1989. Reprinted in *The Cultural Studies Reader.* Ed. Simon During. New York: Routledge, 1993. 135–50.

Spacks, Patricia Meyer. *Gossip*. Chicago: University of Chicago Press, 1986.

Spillers, Hortense J. "Who Cuts the Border?: Some Readings on 'America.'" Introduction to *Comparative American Identities: Race, Sex, and Nationality in the Modern Text*. Ed. Hortense J. Spillers. Essays from the English Institute 1. New York: Routledge, 1991.

Stagg, Jason. E-mail communication. Baton Rouge, Louisiana, March 10, 2000.

Stahl, Sandra Dolby. *Literary Folkloristics and the Personal Narrative*. Bloomington: Indiana University Press, 1989.

———. "Personal Experience Stories." In *Handbook of American Folklore*. Ed. Richard M. Dorson. Bloomington: Indiana University Press, 1983. 268–76.

Stepto, Robert B. *From behind the Veil: A Study of Afro-American Narrative*. 1979. 2nd ed. Urbana: University of Illinois Press, 1991.

Stirling, Frances L. Letter to the author. Baton Rouge, Louisiana, May 2, 1999.

Stone, Elizabeth. *Black Sheep and Kissing Cousins: How Our Family Stories Shape Us*. New York: Penguin, 1989.

Svingen, Kristen. "I'm Swinging into Fame." *Raleigh News and Observer*, August 6, 1999. E1.

Tate, Allen. "A Southern Mode of the Imagination." In *Essays of Four Decades*. Chicago: Swallow Press, 1968. 577–92.

Taylor, Vee. Letter to the author. Zachary, Louisiana, September 23, 1996.

Thomas, Robert R. "Sunday Afternoon with Paw Paw." Unpublished essay, August 1999.

Tittlebaum, Kathleen. Student journal. Louisiana State University, Baton Rouge, November 1998.

Toelken, Barre. *The Dynamics of Folklore*. Boston: Houghton Mifflin Co., 1979.

Traxler, Mary. Personal interview. Baton Rouge, Louisiana, July 15, 1996.

Turner, Lorenzo. *Africanisms in the Gullah Dialect*. 1949. New York: Arno Press, 1968.

Turner, Victor. *Dramas, Fields, and Metaphors: Symbolic Action in Human Society*. Symbol, Myth, and Ritual. Ed. Victor Turner. Ithaca, N.Y.: Cornell University Press, 1974.

Unnamed informant. Personal interview. Baton Rouge, Louisiana, July 12, 1996. Followup by e-mail correspondence, July 16, 1999.

Unnamed informant. Personal interview. Baton Rouge, Louisiana, October 18, 1996.

Unnamed informant. Telephone interview. New Orleans, Louisiana, July 19, 1996.

U.S. Bureau of the Census. *Statistical Abstract of the United States: 1998*. 118th ed. Washington, D.C.: Government Printing Office, 1998.

Veillon, David, II. "Studies of the Porch in My Life." Unpublished student essay. Louisiana State University, Baton Rouge, October 11, 1999.

Villamil, Nena. Student journal. Louisiana State University, Baton Rouge, November 1999.

Vlach, John Michael. *The Afro-American Tradition in Decorative Arts.* Cleveland, Ohio: Cleveland Museum of Art, 1978.

————. *Back of the Big House: The Architecture of Plantation Slavery.* Chapel Hill: University of North Carolina Press, 1993.

————. *By the Work of Their Hands: Studies in Afro-American Folklife.* Charlottesville: University Press of Virginia, 1991.

Walker, Alice. *In Search of Our Mothers' Gardens.* New York: Harcourt Brace Jovanovich, 1984.

Walter, Eugene. "Secrets of a Southern Porch." *New Yorker* (June 22, 1998): 60, 63.

Wells, Marsha. Telephone interview. New Orleans, Louisiana, March 15, 2001.

Wells, Rebecca. *Divine Secrets of the Ya-Ya Sisterhood.* New York: HarperCollins, 1996.

Williams, Michael Ann. *Homeplace: The Social Use and Meaning of the Folk Dwelling in Southwestern North Carolina.* Athens: University of Georgia Press, 1991.

Woestendiek, John. "Tradition or Nuisance?: Ordinance Aims to Curb Porch Furniture." *Sunday Advocate* (Baton Rouge), April 26, 1998. D4.

Women's Community Rehabilitation Center (WCRC). Group interview. Baton Rouge, Louisiana, June 23, 1999.

Wray, Matt, and Annalee Newitz, eds. *White Trash: Race and Class in America.* New York: Routledge, 1997.

INDEX

Absalom, Absalom! (Faulkner), 28, 95–96, 119–20

African Americans: and greeting, 1; and boundaries, 9–11, 19; and porch furniture, 12; and porch use, 18, 50–56, 71–73; as free blacks, 18, 58–59, 73, 74; and storytelling, 26; oral culture of, 38; intraracial divisions among, 51, 73–74; and store porches, 51–53; and architectural porch history, 58, 65; and European culture, 67–68, 69, 78, 79; and African cultural retention, 68–69, 78, 79; dialects of, 69, 78; and class, 73–74; and poor whites, 83–86, 95–96; burial practices of, 89; and "stage Negro," 90–91. *See also* Slavery

Agrarian traditions, 22, 39, 100, 101, 106, 122–23, 140

Air-conditioning: and prevalence of porches, 6, 7, 20, 22, 23–24, 80; and class, 13, 24; and front porches, 90; and porch's role, 99, 160, 169, 176; and community, 102

Alford, Dorothy M., 126–27

Allison, Dorothy: *Bastard Out of Carolina*, 28, 84–86, 95, 132–36, 137, 148–50; *Skin*, 149

Angola tribe, 70

Arawak Indians, 61–62, 65, 67

Architectural porch history: and porch as creolized structure, 15, 28, 67, 71; and race, 57, 58, 67; and European, 58, 62–63, 65; and shotgun houses, 58–59, 61–62; and Haitian immigrants, 58–59, 65; and Yoruba, 59, 61; and porticoes, 96

Architecture: European, 15, 28, 58, 62–63, 65, 67; Caribbean, 15, 65, 67; West Indian, 28, 65

— traditional African: and porch as creolized space, 15, 28; and architectural porch history, 57–59, 61–62, 65, 67

Arsenault, Raymond, 23–24

Aurit, Phil, Jr., 130–31

Automobiles: and front porches, 2; and porch use, 31–34, 37, 39–41, 170; and courtship, 146

Babin, Joyce Hebert, 115

Bailey, Beth, 146

Bartlett, Brother Joe, 112–13

Bastard Out of Carolina (Allison), 28, 84–86, 95, 132–36, 137, 148–50

Baton Rouge, 155–57

Beckham, Sue Bridwell, 14, 15, 20

"Bell Isle: (Central Park of Detroit)" (Hodges), 3–4, 10–11, 42–43

Black English Vernacular, 69

Blessed Assurance (Gurganus), 73

Bohio, 62

Bolsterli, Margaret Jones, 1

Boshamer, Grace Piner, 34, 142

Boundaries: and community, 7–11, 13, 77; and race, 8, 9, 10–11, 13, 18, 19, 28, 57, 80–83, 86, 90–91; and class, 8, 13, 28, 57, 80, 95–97; and genera-

place, 25; and cultural identity, 28; and race, 83; and front porches, 148–49, 151–55; and space, 155, 159; and liminal spaces, 156

Shank, Rebecca Gentry, 35

Shotgun houses, 24, 61–62, 70, 84; Haitian, 15, 58–59

Simeon, Gwen, 92–93

Simpson, Leah Beth, 43–44, 45

Skin (Allison), 149

Slavery: and southern culture, 23; and architectural porch history, 65; and cultural miscegenation, 67; and African culture, 68, 79; and Voodoo, 70; legacy of, 80; and poor whites, 96. See also African Americans

Smith, Lee: Oral History, 18–19

Smoking, 170

Social control: and values, 8; and porch furniture, 12–13; and front porch, 27, 109–10, 141–42, 148, 158; and identity, 41–42, 43, 49; and gossip, 55, 101, 102, 103–4, 105; and cultural limits, 79–80; and men, 116; and courting, 141, 146–47

Soja, Edward, 13

Sophcom, 171–76

Sound and the Fury, The (Faulkner), 27

Space: and children, 6–7, 110–14, 126; creolized space, 15, 17, 28, 67, 71, 88, 92; definition of, 25; and boundaries, 25–26; and power, 25–26, 27, 79, 93, 97; and literary studies, 26–27, 28; and identity, 27, 49, 50, 52–56, 77, 98, 126, 150, 159, 160; and southern culture, 29, 37, 100; social/psychological significance of, 37; and back porches, 55, 56; and courting, 140; and sexuality, 155, 159. See also Liminal spaces; Public/private space

Spacks, Patricia Meyer, 101, 104, 158

Spain, 65

Spanish Town (Baton Rouge), 7, 14–15, 155–57

Stagg, Jason, 82

Stirling, Frances, 20, 111

Stone, Elizabeth, 133

Store porches, 51–53, 54, 55, 146

Storytelling: and porch use, 3–5, 51, 135, 162; and children, 7, 30, 39, 111, 115–16; and front porches, 10, 36, 48; and southern culture, 18, 37, 38–40, 49; and African Americans, 26; porch as metaphor for, 26; and back porches, 47, 51, 54–55; and community, 51–52; and men, 51–52, 115–17, 119, 122; and gossip, 55, 103; and porch swings, 117

Supreme Court, U.S., 84

Svingen, Kristin, 17

Tate, Allen, 37

Taylor, Vee, 36

Television, 13, 22, 24, 160, 169

Their Eyes Were Watching God (Hurston), 50–56, 57, 114

Thomas, Robert R., 116–17

Ti-kay, 59

Tittlebaum, Kathleen, 164

Toussaint L'Ouverture, 58

Traxler, Mary, 147–48

Turner, Lorenzo, 69, 78

Turner, Victor, 13

'Tween porch, 48

Urban planners, 26, 168

Values, 7, 106

Veillon, David, II, 147

Verandas, 15, 59, 61

Villamil, Nena, 165

Visiting: and liminal spaces, 14, 15; and front porches, 35, 44, 45, 99, 104, 123,